Dear É

Thanks so much for your powerful endorsement. I know it will touch many, as it has me. With love, Elsie

THE PATH TO CONTENTMENT

Also written by Elsie Spittle

Wisdom for Life
Our True Identity. . . Three Principles
Beyond Imagination—A New Reality Awaits
Nuggets of Wisdom—Learning to See Them

THE PATH TO CONTENTMENT

ELSIE SPITTLE

Copyright © 2018 Elsie Spittle
ISBN-13: 978-1981551361
ISBN-10: 1981551360
Library of Congress Control Number: 2018901692
CreateSpace Independent Publishing Platform
North Charleston, South Carolina

First printed in 2018
Printed in the USA

Editor: Jane Tucker
Cover design and book layout: Tom Tucker
Cover photo: Elsie Spittle
Author photo: Chris Nunan: http://www.nunan.dk/

Note: All client names are fictitious.

About the Author

Elsie Spittle has been an internationally recognized trainer and consultant for over four decades. She is in the unique position of having known Sydney Banks, originator of the Three Principles, before he had his epiphany. She witnessed the extraordinary change that occurred in him and the unprecedented impact his work had on thousands of people, and how this has brought about a new paradigm in the fields of psychology and psychiatry.

Elsie had the privilege of receiving "on the job" training directly from Mr. Banks, traveling with him to address mental health practitioners, educators, and others seeking a deeper understanding of life. She is considered the first formal teacher of the Principles, after Sydney Banks.

Highly regarded as a public speaker who has the ability to reach audiences, large and small, via a *feeling* that touches the heart and soul, Elsie is also sought out as a mentor by both new and experienced practitioners. She is co-founder of the Three Principles School, based on Salt Spring Island, BC. This is Elsie's fifth published book.

Elsie's website: www.3phd.net

Endorsements
What people are saying about *The Path to Contentment*

"On many occasions, Syd Banks stated that the Three Principles would fundamentally change the fields of Psychology and Psychiatry. This change would occur through a focus on a person's innate mental health, rather than their dysfunction. Elsie Spittle's latest book, *The Path to Contentment* will go a long way in moving Syd's prediction forward.

"Syd Banks often talked about the importance of finding a deep feeling of well-being within as the key to understanding and experiencing the Principles. In reading this compilation of stories and reflections, it is so clear that Elsie lives her life in that beautiful feeling. The brilliance of the book is how she is able to transmit this feeling to the reader. While reading, I felt like I was going on a journey with someone who has a deep understanding of life and of who and what she is—a journey back home, to my True Nature, to a place of joy, peace, and contentment. I have never had an experience quite like this from reading a book. Wow! What a gift!

"I can't wait to recommend this book to my patients and colleagues. If my experience of reading *The Path to Contentment* is any indication of how others will feel, then Elsie Spittle has just made a major contribution to the field of mental health by helping people more deeply appreciate their own innate health and well-being. As I see it, this appreciation is exactly what Syd Banks had in mind when he stated that the Three Principles would fundamentally change the fields of Psychology and Psychiatry. Thank you, Elsie!"

Robert J. Solomon, MD, is an adult, child and adolescent psychiatrist in private practice.

"*The Path To Contentment* leaves the reader feeling hopeful and relaxed. Elsie's new book conveys the deep feeling of simplicity and ease we receive from exploring the Three Principles. We get a deeper insight into the principles behind life, as well as the life of Sydney Banks, paving the way for an easier experience in everything from our relationships to business and health. Each story leaves us feeling closer to Elsie and to Sydney Banks himself, and relaxed enough to feel peace of mind; a shortcut to contentment if ever there was one."

Grace Kelly, Coach & Founder of CityGirlConfidence.com (Winner of the Forbes Top 100 websites for women).

"Elsie Spittle's new book *The Path to Contentment* is Soul Music. It is a gentle, honest, and insightful sharing of the understanding of the three principles and our True Nature. As I read each chapter I felt incredible peace of mind and felt warm feelings of love and understanding rise to the surface.

"As a psychologist, I know that the principles shared in this book offer hope for humanity to find the well-being they are searching for; hope that people can transcend their emotional problems, addictions, and relationship difficulties to discover the love, understanding, and wisdom that insights into the principles uncover ."

Mark Howard, PhD, is recognized as one of the original professionals bringing this understanding to psychology and related fields. In 2008, Mark was granted the "Outstanding Career Service" award by the Santa Clara Psychological Association for his Three Principles work.

"If you are in a helping profession of any kind, Elsie's book, *The Path to Contentment*, will speak to you deeply. Throughout, she shares insights and stories that demonstrate the deeper essence of human nature and the profound results that happen when we help people awaken to this Truth. Elsie has been a mentor, friend and inspiration in my own work and I know her words will do the same for you. Elsie exemplifies the richness we experience when we remain students, look in the direction of our True Nature and let Wisdom reveal itself in the everyday ordinariness of our extraordinary lives."

Barbara Patterson, Global Coach & Consultant, Conversations that Transform

This is what people had to say about Elsie's previous books:

"Elsie Spittle is a treasure—warm and wise with a depth of understanding that illuminates human psychology. In her book, *Nuggets of Wisdom*, she shares hundreds of discreet invitations to awaken to our own ultimate resource—the wealth of wisdom within us."

Michael Neill, radio show host and bestselling author of
The Inside-Out Revolution.

"In *Beyond Imagination* Elsie Spittle shares her improbable journey from housewife to international consultant. Elsie's sharing of the Three Universal Principles, as revealed to her friend Sydney Banks, is done with clarity, warmth, elegance and ease.

"Reading this book will awaken many souls to their 'true identity' and an experience of peace. From that perspective, Elsie's vision of world peace looks not only possible, but likely."

William F. Pettit Jr. MD, Co-owner Three Principles Intervention LLC;
Former Associate Professor of Psychiatry, West Virginia University
School of Medicine.

"In *Our True Identity* Elsie described her first meetings with Sydney Banks, her initial reactions, and how she finally realized the truth behind what he was saying. Elsie draws the reader into an extraordinary story—told in a wonderfully ordinary fashion. Once the reader is quite comfortable, Elsie begins giving actual examples of people who are finding insights from within their own wisdom. This touched me deeply. These stories remind us that beautiful feelings and peace of mind are not dependent on time or circumstances; they do, indeed, exist before time. To the author, I want to say, 'Thank you, thank you, thank you, for writing this book.'"

Gordon Trockman, MD, Psychiatrist, Hawaii.

"Wisdom is not only expressed in words; it reveals itself in the day-to-day living of life. This book, *Wisdom for Life*, provides some great guidance for all of us on the journey of realizing 'the wisdom within.' Elsie offers a great collection of stories and examples of how insight unfolds into a wiser navigation through the everyday business of life."

Tim Foley, Human Resources Executive, International Truck and Engine Corporation.

I'm eternally grateful for Ken, my husband of 55 years. Together we've traveled this extraordinary, mystical journey with an Enlightened man, Sydney Banks. Ken has never faltered in supporting Syd's work. His quiet strength and clear vision in helping to preserve Syd's legacy has bolstered and supported mine countless times. He is the love of my life, the salt of the earth, and adds a lot of spice to my world.

Dedication

To the late Sydney Banks

I'm beyond fortunate to have traveled this extraordinary journey with an Enlightened being; one who was at the same time, ordinary and extraordinary. As a husband, father, friend; ordinary. As a mentor to the world; extraordinary.

CONTENTS

THE THREE PRINCIPLES AS TAUGHT BY SYDNEY BANKS

"Universal Mind is the intelligence of all things, whether in form or formless."
The Enlightened Gardener Revisited.

"Consciousness is the gift of awareness. Consciousness allows the recognition of form, form being the expression of Thought.

"Thought is the missing link that gives us the power to recognize the illusionary separation between the spiritual world and the world of form."

He went on to say:
"The wisdom humanity seeks lies within the consciousness of all human beings, trapped and held prisoner by their own personal minds."
The Missing Link: Reflections on Philosophy & Spirit

Introduction

This book is a compilation of stories and reflections, based on the three spiritual gifts that Sydney Banks uncovered in the early 1970s. He called these gifts: Mind, Consciousness, and Thought. Syd knew these gifts were foundational to the human experience, but it wasn't until later, when the first psychologists came to study with Syd, that they became known as the Three Principles.

Syd's discovery introduced a new paradigm to the fields of psychology and psychiatry. He taught the early psychologists to focus on innate mental health in their clients, rather than paying attention to dysfunction. This was a game changer for mental health professionals.

Not only did a non-professional, an ex-welder, offer a completely new understanding to the service providers, he stated that these Principles would totally change the fields of psychology and psychiatry, in a way never seen before. Thus the Three Principles became known as a new paradigm; offering, for the first time, a cure for mental illness.

On the pages that follow, you will read about the historical context of Syd's profound Enlightenment and its effect upon the field of mental health. A gathering featuring Sydney Banks' work took place at the Scottish Parliament in May, 2015. (Arranged by Jacquie Forde). This historic event was the first time the Three Principles were introduced and acknowledged in any Parliament, anywhere in the world. A panel was invited to discuss the potential for humanity of the Three Principles understanding, while honoring the legacy and message of Mr. Banks, who was born in Edinburgh.

The chapters in this book tell of amazing journeys of inner evolution, of finding a path to contentment that starts "inside" and ends "inside." Although these are individual, stand-alone stories and reflections, there is a consistent thread of understanding binding them together.

It is a book filled with heart and soul; with stories of insight leading to success beyond what could have been imagined; of challenges faced and overcome with love and laughter; of finding contentment after depression.

I hope you enjoy reading as much as I enjoyed sharing.

Author's Note:

I suggest you leisurely read one chapter at a time, leaving space in between for your own insights to emerge. Immerse yourself in the *feeling* of these stories. Because each chapter was written as a stand-alone piece, you may come upon some content that seems familiar from previous pages. This offers an opportunity to *hear* something new, something that adds deeper nuance to the meaning of the story.

CHAPTER 1
THE PROFUNDITY OF BEING ORDINARY

When I first met Sydney Banks in the early '70's, I enjoyed his ordinariness. Syd was a good and kind husband and father, who dearly loved his family. He was an ordinary working man who took pride in his trade as a welder. He would discuss the pros and cons of pulp mill unions with my husband, Ken. Syd had complaints about management and his work, just like Ken did. We were ordinary people doing the best we could with the hand life had dealt us.

We all operated in a basically insecure reality, but we didn't realize it. We didn't know we were insecure. If you would have suggested this to us, I for one would have defended myself quite robustly, and I know Ken would have done the same. The anxiety and unhappiness I often felt was, I believed, normal. I didn't know anything else. And so it went. We felt this was all life had to offer and indeed, both Syd and Ken felt very fortunate to have such good jobs at the local mill.

Then, fate interrupted Syd's life. Profound wisdom was released from within this man's soul. It was life-changing, not only for him, but for the world. In a spontaneous Enlightenment, Syd uncovered three spiritual Principles: Mind, Consciousness, and Thought. These Principles are universal. They are the foundation for humanity's ability to create our own experience, each and every moment.

Syd transformed before our eyes. No longer the insecure person we had felt comfortable with, he was imbued with an authority not of this world. The confidence and certainty he had about what he'd uncovered frightened us. It shook the very foundation of the belief system we had built up over our lifetimes. I resisted his profound message—both Ken and I did—for a long time.

The curious thing was that Syd was still quite ordinary; but the ordinariness was imbued with something unique—a feeling of depth, of unconditional love, of presence. This presence conveyed a level of joy and contentment I had never observed in anyone else, and never before in the man himself. The heartwarming feelings coming from Syd drew us to him, as long as he didn't talk about what he had discovered. When he did, his words threatened our core beliefs. It felt like the rug was being pulled out from under our feet, yet the depth of his feeling comforted us. What a contradiction! A mystery was unfolding before our very eyes.

CHAPTER 2
INSIGHT AND EVOLUTION

After a period of increasing resistance based in my fear of the mystical, and disbelief that an experience such as Syd described could even be possible, I had my own moment of insight. That moment turned my world upside down, and landed me right side up! I had started my journey.

I saw there was something deeper going on inside me. I could *see* the connection between thought and feeling; that when I thought in a certain way, that thought created my experience. I began to realize I had a choice in how I used the spiritual power of Thought; I could use it in a constructive way or in a destructive way.

This discovery filled me with elation, with love, and with hope for the future. For the first time in my life, I felt worthy and filled with purpose. The question I had asked myself for years, "Is this all there is to life? Is this it?" had been answered. I didn't know exactly what my purpose was yet, but I didn't feel empty inside myself any longer.

My life and my relationships with Ken and our children became easier, gentler, with more understanding and less contention. I fell in love with my family in a deeper, unconditional way. Certainly, as time went on, we had our ups and downs, but a trustworthy foundation had been laid in our family relationships.

I also began to get a deeper sense of the extraordinary event that had transpired for Syd, an ordinary working man who had received the ultimate answer humanity has been seeking since time began. Syd told us he had found the secret to life. He calmly stated that the spiritual facts he'd uncovered of Mind, Consciousness, and Thought had the power to change the fields of psychology and psychiatry. My earlier disbelief of these words vanished like mist as the sun rises.

As my life continued to evolve, I could see there was something very special going on because of Syd uncovering these precious

Principles. People from around the world were being drawn to Salt Spring Island to meet with Syd, to study with him and to learn what he'd uncovered. Miracles were happening around us; people from all walks of life were finding their innate wisdom which released their long held mental stress, anxiety and in some cases, deep trauma. This in turn helped heal their physical ailments (in some cases, after many years of medication and fruitless treatment for various medical issues).

Professionals from the mental health field heard of these wondrous stories and began coming to investigate how people could be getting mentally and physically healthy, simply by talking with a non-professional from outside the mental health field—an ex welder, no less! This was intriguing, and needless to say, aroused a good deal of curiosity among the first psychologists who arrived.

As these amazing events continued to occur, Syd would often invite Ken and me to sit in on meetings with the psychologists, who were appearing more frequently on the island. He encouraged us to share our journey with them. We were happy to do so—but there was a bit of a wake-up call that transpired as the professionals began to question us about the changes in ourselves and our family relations, and asking us to share our observations of those who were listening to Syd's teachings. We began to feel special.

One of the things Syd often spoke about was being ordinary. I'd been ordinary all my life, so I wasn't enamored with his direction to *"be ordinary."* He would tell us that once we'd had an insight, to just live, be ordinary, and go about our everyday business. He told us we'd see the world differently; that our many "issues" would become non-issues, that we'd have far more enjoyment with the simple things in life.

I found this a bit perturbing. It's true that my life had changed a great deal, but I was hanging on to the need to feel special, not ordinary. The feeling was subtle; so subtle I didn't see it for a while. Misinterpreting and confusing the Principles' message of hope and transformation with my ego's desire to be something special in this world soon brought me to the realization that being special was an ever-elusive goal. The longer I hung on to that need, the less special I felt. My life once again felt like it was in a tail spin. Go figure!

Chapter 3
Our Divine Birthright

One day as I was wandering down the back road to Syd's place to help him work on his first book, *Second Chance,* I observed a squirrel digging in the soil, diligently scooping through the leaves. He was hiding some nuts he'd found, a treasure for the future. It occurred to me in a flash of insight that I also was hiding a treasure—my innate wisdom. I was covering up my natural wisdom by my ego's need to be special.

That revelation filled me with wonder, lifting my spirits to a height I had not experienced before. My need to feel special evaporated, as if blown away by a gentle puff of wind. I realized we are all born special. From birth to death, we are spiritual beings privileged to create and live in the beautiful form of life.

To realize we have the power to create our personal experience is a very special gift. It is our divine birthright. There is nothing more special than this gift. This knowledge struck me with such depth. I understood for the first time that living an ordinary life, walking down a country lane, could be transformed into a magical journey. As my spirits and level of consciousness lifted, my observations of the physical world around me were enhanced. I'd never before seen such beauty, such a deep dimension of nature. The colors were brighter, richer, enlivened with energy. Nature seemed to shimmer before my eyes.

I arrived at Syd's door, knocked and was invited to enter. Syd gave me a hug as I stood before him. He took one look at my face and grinned from ear to ear. *"Something has happened to you. You look as if you've received a Christmas present and birthday present all rolled into one."*

I shared my experience with him—my need to feel special and how I hadn't liked his encouragement to *"be ordinary."* Telling him about the insight I'd had as I walked down the country lane, and how my vision of the surrounding environment was enriched, I felt overcome with emotion and had to stop.

He chuckled as he listened. *"You've finally entered a whole new world, the mystical world of true knowledge, where everything becomes new again. The most ordinary things in life take on new meaning and you feel new appreciation, both for your surroundings and for your family and friends. Continue to be grateful for what you've just seen and you'll never go wrong. Gratitude is the lubricant for a happy life."*

Those words are imprinted upon my soul. I've never forgotten them and they stand me in good stead to this very day. Gratitude truly is the lubricant for a happy, contented life. And, in being ordinary and acknowledging our divine inheritance, we are, indeed, special.

CHAPTER 4
HAPPY NEW YEAR!

I hope your year is filled with insightful learning. The passing of the old year and the arrival of the new brings opportunity to put to bed previously held beliefs and to be open to something new, especially spiritual facts about who and what we really are.

What will the change be? Perhaps a medical condition that we need to address. Perhaps new ways of seeing familiar relationships. Financial concerns may be an issue. A new job may be in our future. Maybe new technology that we need to learn. Whatever the change is, there is an easier way to *see* change when you have the Three Principles as a foundation of understanding.

All of these changes used to be stressful for me. I dreaded change. Now, I look forward to change; I embrace it, knowing that new learning adds vitality to one's life, if you are open to it. If you *see* that we actually create reality, using the Three Principles of Mind, Consciousness and Thought, you will be able to flow through the mechanism of change with grace and ease. Being closed to change, whatever that may look like, is what makes it difficult.

I know challenges arise in one's life and it may not be easy to adapt. But if we see that life is not static and change is always occurring, it helps a great deal. If you can connect the flow of change to the flow of spiritual energy which is never still but always in motion, it helps ease the path. We may not understand why a certain situation is happening, but if we take a step back, our innate wisdom has a chance to emerge, once again shining the light of understanding on the "why's" and "why not's" of life.

I've not always been a patient person; I like to get things done. . . and move forward. Sometimes that impatience has gotten in my way, where I've expected more from others and judged when things haven't gone according to plan. I don't like the feeling of judgment.

I have found that as I've uncovered more of my true nature, the highest part of me, I've also uncovered more patience; more patience to let life show me what my best learning is. Is change always what I hope for or expect? Not at all; but I always learn from change now that I've let patience and understanding guide me.

This is what I wish for the world—more patience and understanding with each other; more love to grow in harmony, working together hand in hand for the betterment of society. We hold the reins in our hands, the means to pass on a better world for future generations. Let's join together to help this happen.

CHAPTER 5
TEMPERING JUDGMENT

It's human nature to judge—or is it? I certainly used to think so, and readily indulged in my judgmental thoughts about others. It didn't feel good, but I felt justified in thinking these thoughts because of the behavior I observed. Blaming the person I was judging for the fact that I didn't feel good didn't help me feel better. Not understanding the role of thought in creating my personal experience made me a victim of my thoughts.

I didn't see the psychological innocence in people. I didn't see that we all do the best we can, given the state of our thinking in the moment. I saw life through the eyes of my thinking. Now I see life much of the time through the eyes of love and understanding.

We all have judgmental thoughts at some point. We may recognize this and rationalize it by pointing to the behavior of the person or people we are judging. However, even when someone has done something wrong, in our eyes, it is enormously helpful to find that quiet, wise place inside where compassion resides. Perhaps there are reasons for the behavior that are not visible to us. And even if we see the reasons but they are not appropriate in our eyes, who are we to judge another? Does it feel good? Does it feel healthy? Does the judgmental thinking bring understanding? If not, then our judgment is not serving us well.

Compassion lifts judgmental thoughts so one can begin to *see* what lies beneath the behavior. Compassion tempers judgment and brings about a deeper understanding of how the Principles of Mind, Consciousness and Thought work in unison, to create reality. Compassion brings out the best in us so we can see the best in others. Compassion brings peace of mind. Compassion is the expression of our True Nature.

CHAPTER 6
GENTLE ON OUR MINDS

My last chapter spoke to the judgment we occasionally feel about other people, and how to temper judgmental thoughts by going inside, where compassion resides. All too often, we can be more judgmental about ourselves than we are with others. It's equally important to be gentle with ourselves. Judging ourselves for what we do or don't do doesn't do any good. Now that's a mouthful, isn't it? I'm simply trying to say that our ability to think is always going to be in play as long as we live. So it makes sense to understand what's in operation behind the scenes.

The Three Principles are spiritual formless energy, manifested into form by our thinking. As we begin to get a glimmer of the spiritual nature of the Principles, this glimmer opens the door to understanding that formless energy is not static—it flows. We have a thought and the next moment the thought moves on—unless we hold it in our minds. When we hold thoughts in our mind in a fixed position, we turn thought into form, and into experience.

We are gifted with the power to use thought to create our personal experience. Logically, it seems reasonable that when we understand the dynamics of thought, we use this capacity to create a mentally healthy experience. However, as you know, we don't always use the power of thought wisely. We often use it against ourselves, creating feelings and experiences that don't serve us well.

The other day I listened to an early tape of Sydney Banks. He talked about how even the most enlightened person could still have negative feelings, that these feeling are always available to all of us. He said that once we realized this, it would give us great freedom because we wouldn't be fighting against those feelings but accepting that they are still available, that we are human as well as spiritual beings. The freedom comes from *realizing* we have a choice.

When I heard that statement, it gave me immediate relief. It helped me see once again the innocence in myself and consequently, to see more clearly the innocence in others. We aren't perfect in the world of form. The game of life is to uncover our true identity, our perfect being that resides within us all. Therein lies the secret; the secret to living in a contented state that allows for the occasional bump to remind us we are students first, and teachers second.

Our journey in discovering our birthright is a continual adventure, sometimes filled with contentment, sometimes challenging. The best way to travel is to enjoy the journey, bumps and all!

CHAPTER 7
SHARING WISDOM

The group conference calls I've been facilitating have just concluded. I'm thrilled with the response and the learning that occurred for all of us, for the participants and for me as host on the calls.

I had been moved to offer people the opportunity to see they had more wisdom inside, and could live more deeply in that wisdom if they acknowledged and shared their innate gift of true knowledge.

From the beginning of Sydney Banks' public teaching, he encouraged us to share the insights we were learning. He told us clearly that to continue our inner evolution we needed to share what we'd learned. He said we needed to empty the vessel in order to refill with new understanding. I saw the truth of that in my own life and wanted to share it with others.

This conference series was different from any I'd offered before. Prior to that, the usual format had been for the group to do more listening to the host, rather than sharing what they knew or were learning in the moment.

Some of the early feedback I received from a few on the new series indicated there was some hesitancy about sharing their wisdom – they preferred to listen to the host. However, once participants began to share their insights, the deep feeling that accompanies insight blossomed and callers were very moved by the group's wisdom.

On the last call, I wanted to hear from some of the participants who hadn't talked before, so I asked one individual if he would care to share whatever was relevant to him. There was a rather lengthy silence. Realizing I'd put this person on the spot by calling on him when I'd assured people that they could talk only when they wanted to, I apologized.

My thoughts took me to what I'd done "wrong" and I felt bad

for a few moments. Then the individual came on the line and explained he'd had trouble unmuting himself so he could offer his comments. Whew! What a relief! I was so delighted, not only by the wise comments he shared, but by the fact that he'd wanted to talk but couldn't unmute. Once again, the power of my thoughts creating my reality in the moment gave me, and I suspect others on the call, new insight into our creative ability.

I recall another incident on a previous series when I was very new to the technology of the conference calling system. Everyone was muted at the beginning, except for me as the host. I was deeply moved by the feeling that emerged as I was sharing new insights with the group. I paused for a moment as a profound quiet overcame me. After a time, I asked for comments or questions from the group. There was utter silence. I thought to myself, "How beautiful. Everyone is as moved as I am by the beautiful stillness of spiritual energy."

I continued to wait for someone else to speak. The silence stretched out. My thoughts began to dart about. Was it possible I was misreading the group's deep listening? Had they hung up on me? Once again I asked for comments. Nothing. . . I heard a knock on my office door. My husband poked his head in and said, "Edward called on the other line to tell you that you've double muted people on the call and they can't unmute themselves! He wanted to share but couldn't."

Oh my word! I burst into laughter as I realized what had happened and quickly corrected the technical situation. We continued the call, and I left it to the others to carry on while I listened. I must admit I'd lost the feeling in the moment and was happy to "mute" myself. The callers found the whole situation very amusing, as did I once I'd settled down.

Later, I got an email from a participant who'd had a completely different experience during our "double muted" call. He thought I'd deliberately let the silence continue so that people could go deeper into their own wisdom during the quiet time I'd offered. Same situation—totally different experience created by our individual thinking, using the spiritual power of Thought.

It never ceases to amaze me how we use the Principle of Thought to create. It's such a natural ability that often times we don't even realize what's happening. We attribute the experience to the external situation that is occurring, rather than to the power we have to think and create. This power is truly a mystical gift!

I would like to end this chapter with a comment from a participant on the calls who is a dear friend and respected colleague. I feel blessed by her friendship. "Everyone who has spoken seems to have picked up on the very deep and sacred feeling of the calls. Way less talk about Mind, Thought and Consciousness as form, more attention focused on before their formation. The mystical nature of the Principles was where everyone was able to go and it was a blessing to spend more time dwelling in the feeling that truly is the essence of the trinity of the Principles."

CHAPTER 8
THE PRACTICALITY OF INNATE WISDOM

First of all, for those who come across this chapter and may be new to this understanding, I'd like to explain something about innate wisdom, in terms of the Three Principles that the late Sydney Banks introduced to the world in 1973. Syd's epiphany revealed three foundational Principles: Mind, Consciousness, and Thought. These Principles underlie the human experience and explain how we create our own personal reality.

Along with these Principles, Syd educated people about the innate wisdom within each of us. He told us that it is simply a matter of *seeing* this spiritual fact that allows this capacity to be released and employed in our everyday life. I have seen this for myself and witnessed it in others.

Let me say this again: Innate wisdom is a spiritual fact—it's not just an idea or concept.

At the same time that wisdom is of spiritual essence, wisdom is also extremely practical. When I first began to learn about the Principles, my impression was that wisdom was something gained with age or learned through experience. Yet at the same time, I saw that people keep making the same mistakes over and over again. If wisdom was gained through aging or experience, why would this happen? It didn't make sense to me.

Over time, as I began to *see* more about the inner workings of my mind, I could see wisdom come to life for me and guide me in my day to day living. It was a natural outcome of simply enjoying my life and not trying to figure everything out with my intellect. I discovered that the more I lived in the present, the more wisdom was released from inside me so that it became my companion and help-mate.

Here is an example. When I started to edit my new book, I had the main body, short stories written over the last few years, but I needed a beginning and an end. Being a writer was something I had never anticipated—it just happened. I had stories to share, and writing was a means of expressing those stories. I never planned on writing a book; I just wrote what was in my heart in the moment.

As I began to review my material, I could see that the articles I'd written lacked continuity when I joined them together. Because I write in the moment about what is meaningful to me at that specific time, I may have written a story about the early days of our spiritual journey with Syd. Then the next article might be about an experience or insight that occurred with a client.

I wasn't sure how to move things around to connect all the stories together, and felt a little overwhelmed. Then I decided to just carry on with my day and do whatever came my way. As I relaxed and just lived, I was drawn back to my computer and the book. As I reviewed again, insight came about how to shift the material around to create continuity. Wisdom was guiding me in a very real, practical sense, and the book flowed together.

It means a great deal to me as an author to be able to count on my best friend, wisdom. Not stressing out about how to edit or write provides a stable mental environment for wisdom and clarity to be released, for me to enjoy my work and to write well and with deep feeling. I've written four books now (this one is my fifth) and I've co-authored two. It's an absolute joy.

I have no doubt that if you reflect for a moment or two, you can recall an example in your own life of times when you've had a challenge to meet, mulled over what to do, finally gave it up for a time, and then had insight come to you about how to meet the challenge. Natural wisdom comes spontaneously when we need it. It's so valuable to know that the more we trust our innate wisdom, the more we benefit from its guidance.

CHAPTER 9
A PRECIOUS GIFT

As I've been working on my book about our journey with Sydney Banks, I've been amazed at the forgotten memories that have come alive. So many historic events took place as Syd shared the spiritual gift he'd uncovered, the Three Principles, with the world.

We witnessed many occasions when Syd spoke to mental health professionals, self-awareness gurus, business leaders, educators, and countless others. Syd knew that if they heard him, their lives would be enriched beyond imagination, and in turn they would guide their clients and employees to contented and productive lives.

Syd shared his profound insight without hesitation, with passion, utmost integrity, and with simplicity. He often called the spiritual facts he'd uncovered a precious gift. Syd humbly gave this gift to the world.

He started by sharing his new found wisdom with his family, then with the people he worked with, and his friends. As time went on, Ken and I considered ourselves to be very fortunate, indeed, to be among Syd's friends, and to travel this amazing journey with him.

Although we didn't understand what had happened to him, and, as mentioned previously, strenuously resisted his message at first, we did feel the experience he'd had was significant. He had an undeniable certainty that the Principles he'd uncovered "*would change the fields of psychology and psychiatry.*" This statement completely baffled us. We felt it was unbelievably arrogant. How could he know such a thing? Furthermore, what gave him the confidence to voice this statement?

We knew from our past experience with Syd, that he had limited education. He was not a reader, had not studied philosophy, psychology, or any "new-age" thinking. Yet he had the confidence to state, unequivocally, that these Principles would not only change the orientation of the mental health field by pointing people to their innate wisdom, but that in doing so, it would naturally help alleviate the suffering of those in need.

Syd was not a seeker. As he put it, "*I didn't know there was anything to find.*" This fact is extremely relevant historically. It illustrates that the profound epiphany Syd experienced happened spontaneously. He was the first proof of the pudding, in a manner of speaking. His epiphany proves innate wisdom exists. Where else could all this new found knowledge he was sharing come from?

Syd also was very clear that everyone has the same capacity for natural wisdom and mental health. No one has any more or any less. We are all born of the same spiritual essence that is the source of natural wisdom and well-being.

Allow me to put into historical context the relevance of the first psychologists arriving on Salt Spring Island. They came to investigate the stories they were hearing about this unknown, modest Scotsman, who apparently was having amazing results helping people find their mental and physical well-being.

Their arrival was the beginning of a completely new paradigm being introduced to the mental health field, focused on the Principles and innate wisdom, rather than dysfunction and techniques.

Not only was this new understanding an incredible evolution in mental health, beyond the realm of traditional modalities that were being taught in universities across the globe at that time, but it was introduced to the professional community by a non-professional. This was an extraordinary situation.

It was many years later, as the landmark significance of this event became clearer to us all, that Dr. George Pransky called it a "defining moment" in the history of psychology.

Dr. Pransky was one of the first psychologists who came to Salt Spring, with his wife and business partner Linda, along with Dr. Roger Mills. In 1978 in the San Francisco Bay area, George and Linda established the first ever Three Principles-based clinic. Dr. Mills became a pioneer in community development, using the Principles as the foundation of his work.

The Three Principles paradigm, as defined and taught by Sydney Banks, is bringing hope and peace of mind to those in great need, letting them know there is a solution to their suffering. This gentle, yet revolutionary understanding is helping many thousands of people in nations around the world, to find their natural well-being and the hidden genius that emerges as a result.

This was Syd's greatest wish: to help alleviate humanity's suffering. He *knew* the Three Principles hold the answer.

Little did we know that the precious gift Syd offered humanity would ultimately sweep across the world, often times, seemingly under the radar. Yet the impact of his revelation would not only continue to stir and awaken peoples' souls, his teachings would be adapted into countless books, curriculums, videos, and so on.

In May of 2015, a historic gathering took place at the Scottish Parliament, featuring Syd's work. A panel was invited to discuss the potential for humanity of The Three Principles understanding, while honoring the legacy and message of Sydney Banks, who was born in Edinburgh. This was the first acknowledgment of the Three Principles that took place in any Parliament, anywhere in the world.

If you haven't checked out Syd's website yet or read his books, I strongly encourage you to do so. His materials have a purity that is unique and has the power to touch one's soul. The more you view his DVDs or read his books, the more you learn. They always evoke new insights. It's a very mystical process that refreshes, supports, and sustains your learning.

CHAPTER 10
BEYOND HABITS OF THOUGHT

Recent conversations I've had with friends and clients have left me reflecting on how powerful Thought is. The Principle of Thought gives us the ability to create our experience from moment to moment. When we are unaware of this, we can become victims of our own thinking.

Recalling my first vacation many years ago brought out a wealth of memories, and laughter at how little I was able to enjoy my holiday. My limited knowledge of how my thinking shaped my experience contributed to my limited capacity to enjoy life.

Ken and I had been invited to accompany Syd and his late wife, Barb, (who passed in 1987) to Hawaii. We were thrilled at the idea; at the same time, we were very nervous at the thought of getting on a plane. Neither of us had ever flown before and we had strong reservations. The "carrot on the stick" that prompted us to go beyond our habitual, fearful thinking was the honor it was to go with Syd.

When I was growing up, vacations were not something my family did. My parents were hard working farmers, without the time, inclination, or financial resources to go on vacation. It just wasn't part of our reality. Life wasn't really meant to be enjoyed. Life was often endured. So I had habits of thought concerning life in general, and specifically, thoughts about holiday breaks, firmly ingrained in my brain by my upbringing. That was natural to my way of being.

On the first holiday in Hawaii, there came a moment when I'd had enough happiness, and with my limited capacity for enjoyment, couldn't take any more good times. So I picked a fight with Ken. Given that Ken was in the same insecure frame of mind, he obliged, and off we were, to the land of tension.

When we'd get together with Syd and Barb for lunch or to stroll on the beach, the tension between Ken and me was hard to miss.

Syd felt it right away, and in his kind manner would ignore it, and simply carry on enjoying his day. If our stress became too obvious, he would end up going off on his own with Barb and leave us to our own devices. I can't say I blamed him. . . .

Syd seldom talked about problems, ours or anyone else's. He knew the best way to help people was to be an example of well-being, to live in the moment with appreciation and enjoyment, and that feeling would touch the soul of anyone in his presence. The feeling that came through Syd was one of compassion, humor, and total understanding of where our state of mind was, and how best to help us move past our habitual thinking, to the world of peace and contentment. He knew that when we calmed down, our innate wisdom would rise to the surface, and once again, guide us on our inner journey.

And sure enough, toward the end of our holiday, as we became more accustomed to the beauty of the Hawaiian island, we began to feel safe and comfortable. Our insecurity was swept away, as if by the trade winds. We loved our few remaining days and had the best time. That experience taught us a lot about how to go beyond our habits of thought.

As I began to get more in touch with my True Self, I was able to utilize the power of Thought with more wisdom, naturally. My capacity for well-being expanded beyond what I had been able to experience before. My five senses were enhanced in ways that brought more joy and satisfaction to my life. My surroundings looked more beautiful, food tasted better than ever, my relationships were more loving; everything changed as my habitual, insecure thinking lessened. I was living in a whole new world, a world of infinite possibility.

CHAPTER 11
THE POWER OF A MOMENT

The simplicity and impact of the Principles can be so subtle that we may sometimes feel we aren't reaching people as much as we would like to. Perhaps as a leader in an organization, caught up in the daily grind, we forget the power of a moment of true communication with another soul.

When we operate from a calm demeanor, just passing someone in the hallway, seeing they are upset, and taking a moment to listen can be very helpful.

We may stop and chat with a check-out clerk at the pharmacy, when we see she is weary. A smile crosses her face as she is touched by the kind human connection. She feels seen and validated as important in life.

The words "Thank you," given to a crossing guard ushering children across a busy street, brings a nod of recognition of kindness extended to a stranger. Kindness lifts the spirit, and it radiates into the world.

A moment is timeless and can offer respite, a moment of peace, a moment of clarity. An insight takes a moment and can change your life. It is wise not to dismiss the power of a moment, but to embrace, cherish, and cultivate more moments of power.

Chapter 12
Walk a Mile in My Shoes

Before I knew about the role of thought in creating reality, I used to harbor ill feelings about certain things people did to me. At least, I *thought* they did it to me. I didn't know it was my thinking about the situation that created the feelings I experienced.

For example: if someone was disrespectful to me, I took it personally, not seeing that the person might be thinking the same thing about me—that I was being inconsiderate toward them. If both of us were thinking the other was being inconsiderate, is it any wonder that our interaction would be less than healthy?

When a quiet moment occurred in my mind, I realized that my thinking was making me a victim of my thoughts. I didn't like the feeling. This was the wake-up call, alerting me to the spiritual fact that we all have the power to create our moment to moment experience.

I have so much respect for that knowledge. It has turned my life around. No matter how real my experience feels, if the feeling is negative, I know something is off track—my thinking.

Even when the situation seems to deserve a response, the negative feeling doesn't justify going to that level to resolve the issue. Far better to calm down, let wisdom emerge, and then take a look with fresh eyes. You'll be surprised how that changes your vision, and your behavior.

Wisdom brings the feeling of compassion—not only for the other individual—but equally important, for yourself. You see the psychological innocence in yourself and in others. We are all doing the best we can, given our thinking in the moment.

Wisdom gives a whole new meaning to the phrase "Walk a mile in my shoes." The moment you metaphorically walk in another person's reality, you see their side in a way you didn't before; you see with understanding why they're acting as they are. And you feel compassion.

The feeling of compassion brings simplicity and solace to the soul. This is where I want to live. How about you?

CHAPTER 13
THE FEELING OF OUR TRUE NATURE

Recently I had the privilege of speaking to hundreds of people in England and Spain, at several different venues. The audience was comprised of people who had varying levels of understanding of the Three Principles, as well as some who were completely new to this innovative paradigm. What struck me the most, and has continued to resonate since my return home, is that it didn't matter. New, familiar, or somewhere in between—all were moved by the feeling of their true nature emerging in the moment.

The focus of my talks, whether I spoke alone, or co-presented with a colleague, was on recognizing our true nature, our inner spiritual core. Everyone seemed to have a sense of this, whether they'd ever heard about the Principles or not. The proof of this was the fact that the *feeling* welled up inside them during the talks. Many participants came up to me afterwards, often in tears, and asked in wonder, "Is this feeling that's coming up inside me my true nature? Is this what you're talking about? I've never felt it before." Others said, "I've never felt this feeling so strongly."

I could see their faces change as the feeling overcame them; they looked as if they'd lost years of stress, lines of worry vanishing from their faces. It was as if they'd had a face lift, a spiritual face lift. Many told me the next day that they were seeing life differently, with less judgment, with more love and understanding. They told me they weren't taking things as personally, that they could see people were doing the best they could, given their attitude toward life.

It moved my heart and soul not only to see the physical evidence of change emerging, but to hear of practical results. The combination of the profound and the practical has always resonated with me.

The *feeling* of our true nature was felt by all. As a speaker, I felt it as I was sharing my understanding. The audience responded, thus contributing and building the overall feeling in the room. It was very a mystical and powerful time.

This amazing feeling of well-being stilled the intellect, and opened the doors, not only to the positive feeling inside, but to the natural wisdom that resides within each soul. The understanding of this spiritual process is the gift Sydney Banks left us, when he uncovered the Three Principles of Mind, Consciousness, and Thought.

Encouraged and moved by witnessing recognition and acknowledgment of our true nature by so many people, I relate this story in the hope that some of the readers, who may be unfamiliar with their own true nature, are touched and curious. I encourage you to explore the work of Sydney Banks and the Three Principles. Our spiritual birthright is waiting to be embraced. Truly, this is a timeless gift for everyone.

Chapter 14
Can Long Term Relationships Still Be Exciting?

A young friend asked me this question after I had shared with her that my husband Ken and I celebrated our golden wedding anniversary several years ago. She looked surprised, and then gave me a loving hug as she extended her congratulations. With a quizzical look, she asked, "Can long term relationships still be exciting? I can't imagine after fifty years together that there's anything left to learn about one other. Haven't you gotten sick of each other?"

I burst into laughter at her direct and earnest inquiry and reached out to give her a cuddle. "There were times in our early marriage when I thought the same thing. I couldn't envisage staying married to one person for fifty years. And yet here we are, together now for fifty-four years; closer than ever and loving one another."

Her question prompted some thoughtful reflection for me. It's not that Ken and I haven't had difficulties from time to time, but that just tempered and strengthened our relationship, bringing about more love and respect for each other.

A significant turning point in our relationship occurred after I had been traveling with Syd, sharing what I'd been learning, at seminars and retreats, universities, mental health centers, and so on. At first, I was humbled and honored by the opportunity to learn in this way, experiencing "on the job training" with Syd. Then it went to my head and my ego had a field day.

I tried to teach the Principles at home, especially to my husband. If he was in a low mood, I would simply tell him, "It's just your thinking." And if that didn't work to help elevate his feeling, I would find some other tidbit of wisdom to feed him. He wasn't hungry for my tidbits. . .

He wanted a wife, a partner, not a teacher. I completely misread the situation and the game was on. We both became entrenched in our own story and ultimately we separated for six months. Ken left the island and moved to the big city; I remained on the island with the children. For a while, it felt easier to be apart because there wasn't the constant tension. But underlying that was the dread of divorce.

During this time, I was working with Syd on his book, *Second Chance*. This gave me great solace. Sometimes I would arrive at his home in tears, filled with angst about the way things were with Ken. Syd would give me a hug, then say, "Let's get to work. Here's another chapter for you to type." And I would find myself drawn into another world, freed from my problems.

As time went on, Ken had contact with the children and I went to stay with him one weekend. But nothing changed, so finally I felt it was time to end the separation and file for divorce. I felt humiliated, the first couple in the Principles community to divorce. That old ego was once again in charge.

When I approached a lawyer on the island, a mutual friend of Ken and myself, to draw up the paperwork, he looked at me in disbelief, and refused. "Grow up, Elsie!" I was hurt and upset by his words and left his office feeling bereft.

I let Syd know what I was planning and he pondered for a moment, then asked if I thought Ken would talk with him. Remember that Ken and Syd worked together at the pulp mill for many years, but during our separation, Ken had pulled away from our friends. I gave him Ken's phone number.

Syd took the ferry and Ken met him at the terminal. They walked and talked on the beach. Neither divulged to me what they spoke of, other than Ken saying that Syd told him, "*You'll always be my buddy, no matter what.*" This meant a great deal to Ken.

Ken came home, and we started again. The only advice Syd gave us was not to go into the past. Sometimes we both had to bite our tongues in order not to do so.

I'd like to say that after that, we fell in love again, and our life together was like a bed of roses. But it wasn't. It took some time before we settled into a new relationship. We fell in "respect." Both of us had a fresh appreciation for the commitment we had to our marriage, to each other, and to our children. That respect turned into a deeper love than either of us had ever experienced before. More trust, more patience, more kindness.

There came a point where our relationship seemed to feed and nourish itself, through understanding that behavior is not the real issue in building and sustaining connection.

As I see it, the most important factor in supporting long term relationships, or any relationship for any length of time, is to know who we truly are, inside. By that, I mean recognizing our spiritual identity, our true nature. When we get a glimmer of the world beyond the form of life, we gain more understanding of what's creating the form—the Principles—used by us to the best of our ability. This knowledge brings less attachment to the form of behavior. It's behavior that usually gets us in trouble in our relationships.

When I became conscious of how we create our experience in life, and that we have a choice in how we think, I found I was more forgiving of myself and not so judgmental. Consequently, I also found myself more forgiving of other people, including of things that I perceived Ken did. It ceased to matter as much who was right and who wasn't. The feeling of love and understanding became our guide; it helped us to step back and regain perspective.

This had a huge impact on our relationship. We used to focus on *who* was right. Our thoughts at that point were very compelling and very real to us. We would both become entrenched in our thinking and conflict would arise.

I remember talking to Syd about this and he suggested we wait until we'd calmed down to discuss sensitive topics. At that time, I felt Syd was telling us to avoid the issue. . . when in reality, he wasn't saying that at all. He was simply advising us to wait until the feeling was more amenable to discussion. Without any understanding, waiting until we were calm definitely looked to me like avoidance. Does this sound familiar?

However, as my wisdom surfaced more of the time, my interest shifted to keeping the positive feeling alive in our relationship. It's not that I ignored certain issues that cropped up; it was a matter of timing. Clearly, when a couple is in the midst of upset, that's not the best time to resolve or discuss matters of concern. When you come together in love, calm and clarity are prevalent. From this position, resolution becomes obvious. We made the journey together; not always at the same time, but still on the same journey, comfortable with our own individual paces.

Over the years, I have seen Ken become more loving and kind, more tender in his response to me, more open to sharing his deeper feelings. His humor has become spontaneous and readily available. He comes out with new thoughts that are fascinating to me and the conversations we have are rich and rewarding. He tells me the same thing; that we both have become more loving and gentle toward one another, and to the world in general.

As we evolve in love and understanding, we have more patience with one another's shortcomings, focusing instead on each other's strengths; this naturally enhances and deepens our relationship.

It enriches our relationship to the global community as well. We find ourselves living more of the time in a world of harmony, with renewed zest for life. We see that this feeling of well-being is contagious and impacts those around us.

So, my answer to my young friend is, "Yes, long term relationships really can continue to be vital, loving, and exciting; the fountain of youth exists in the feeling of love."

CHAPTER 15
TIPS FOR MAINTAINING WELL-BEING

* Be gentle with yourself! It is absolutely natural that you can't be strong all the time. You are not superwoman/superman...when you try so hard to be perfect, you leave no room for understanding and acceptance of what is.

* Just live—enjoy life every moment. That is hope in action.

* Observe "Ping-Pong" thoughts—just notice and don't judge. Remember that ability to notice is the Principle of Consciousness in action.

* Trust yourself and don't futurize. We don't know what the future holds—if we live in the moment, the future will take care of itself, far better than we can.

* Don't try and change the world. Change your view of the world and the world will change; maybe not in the way you anticipate, but in the way the Universe is meant to be.

* Be thankful for what you have now, in this moment. Gratitude is the best lubricant in the world for maintaining well-being.

* Remember, we are all One, doing the best we can as spiritual beings living in a material world. This is the game called life; let's play it to the best of our ability.

CHAPTER 16
SAFE AND PROTECTED BY WISDOM

As I was out on my morning walk, enjoying the satisfying crunch of fallen autumn leaves underfoot, I noticed an unusual sight in the meadow by the road. I stopped to gaze more fully and realized I was looking at two deer, ears perked up at attention, viewing me as I was staring at them. Their bodies were completely enclosed by their natural environment, the long grass in the field. Only their heads were visible. They were largely protected from natural predators, and could leap away if danger appeared.

The scene brought a smile to my face and I thought, "What a parallel to our wisdom, to the Principles nestled inside of us." We are protected by our true nature just as the deer are protected, only more so. We are the Principles in action. Understanding this empowers us. Wisdom is released, and brings safety into our world; a protective factor, insulating us from the stress and chaos that can occur as part of life.

The Principles of Mind, Consciousness and Thought are always working within us, whether we know it or not; whether we feel caught up in our worries or not. We are always using the Principles. The only distinction is when we are using them as they are meant to be used—to live a fulfilling, satisfying life, filled with purpose and service to others—or using them against ourselves by creating worry, anxiety, and so forth.

When our bodies and souls are protected by wisdom, stress seems to pass us by, just as natural dangers bypass the deer, protected within their natural environment.

Seeing life through the eyes of our true nature helps us move through the various experiences we have with grace and gratitude. This way of seeing life results in less judgment of ourselves and others, and more kindness and humor.

CHAPTER 17
INSIGHT IS ALWAYS AVAILABLE

In the flash of an insight, we gain some understanding of how we create reality, and it becomes obvious to us that we are in charge; we are the "thinker." Then, life throws us a curve and our contented life doesn't look quite as promising. Life no longer appears as rich and inviting. Our understanding is not as clear. Our ego and intellect come into play and hang on for dear life; old patterns of thought and behavior reappear.

This is rather unnerving, to say the least. It's a big pain in the "you know what." Here we were, evolving quite nicely, at peace and enjoying our experience of life; then it seems to come out of nowhere; resistance blocks our pathway. What's most unsettling is that it's our own resistance, coming from our own thinking! And we thought we knew better. . .

It seems to me that Universal Mind has a cosmic sense of humor, not always understood by the human part of us. When Syd Banks would talk about life being a *"contact sport,"* I thought I understood that phrase. Those two words continue to unfold and provide new meaning in my life.

This is the duality of our spiritual nature and our human nature playing the game of life. Each unfolding and connecting, helping us to discover there is no duality—only formless energy playing both roles.

To return to well-being, it's helpful to clear the deck, so to speak, to quiet our mind so wisdom can once again emerge and guide us. However, it's not essential. What I've also seen is that even when our mind isn't quiet, wisdom can come through the fog of our personal thinking to bring new understanding.

This happened to me. In the midst of great angst, wisdom pierced the veil of confusion and I had my first insight. I know this has happened with others as well.

Reflect on your life; I'm sure you've had times when life seemed wrought with worry; then a shift happened and all of a sudden, things weren't so bad. You've had an "Ah-ha" moment.

As I continue to gain clarity on this spiritual fact, that insight can happen at any time because it's already within us, I find I'm not so bothered when I'm thrown a curve. I know it's just temporary and that learning is taking place.

I'm so grateful for this. Knowing not to stress over the roadblocks, knowing that as the orientation of our thinking shifts from what's wrong to what's right, so does our experience.

Once more, we experience the Three Principles working in unison to create our reality... Once more, wisdom is holding our hand as we traverse through small and large roadblocks of life... Once more, we are finding peace of mind and contentment within.

CHAPTER 18
THE ILLUSIONARY NATURE OF REALITY

The evolution of our understanding, as practitioners, of how reality is created via thought is quite remarkable. I've observed that as we more fully acknowledge the deeper essence or truth behind life, we see this reflected in our impact on clients; on how powerful the transformation is, how simple the "cure."

Becoming more aware of the illusionary nature of life is a natural outcome of wisdom being released from within. It feels like one "slips" into another reality, with such ease and naturalness, that often one is oblivious to this new reality until all of a sudden, Bingo! You *see* that how you used to view and feel about life has shifted.

In the early days of Syd's teaching, when he would speak about "*the energy of all things*," this phrase went over my head. I felt it, and strongly sensed an underlying meaning, but couldn't wrap my intellect around it. It eluded my understanding.

One thing that became clear in my journey was that thought creates feeling. I discovered that when I thought one way about a subject, that thinking brought about certain feelings and behavior. When my thinking changed, so did my experience.

For example, my critical thinking about joining Facebook prevented me from seeing the advantages of sharing the Principles with a wider population via the social media network. Then, my thinking changed and I saw the enormous potential for offering hope and an answer to life's dilemmas, to those who don't know they are the thinker.

The before picture was my stubbornness in refusing to even consider joining FB. The after picture was a happy face, delighted with the opportunity to connect with friends, colleagues, and new people throughout the world.

I used to linger and focus on the thinking that brought about the change—the change in the form of experience. I found the change fascinating and freeing from my "stuck" beliefs. But I also found the focus on thinking could tie me to that thinking, rather than opening my mind to the power we have, via thought, to create.

Then one day I began to *see* beyond the before-and-after picture of experience. In the past, this focus on my thinking would entice me to try and figure out how change happened. Before I knew it, I would be immersed in my thinking and would have lost the *feeling* of change, the *feeling* of the formless energy behind life. When one's mind is filled with thinking, there is no room for wisdom to emerge, no room for the evolution of the human spirit.

As I began to be intrigued by the illusionary nature of experience, I could see that change was evidence; evidence of the illusionary nature of reality. How can reality change if it isn't formless energy, continually changing shape via our power to think?

The conversation that took place in my soul encompassed Mind, Consciousness, and Thought: Insights come from Mind. Awareness of the insights come from Consciousness. Reality takes form through the power of Thought.

The human spirit is irrevocably connected to our spiritual being; when we embrace our true nature, life is filled with more ease, more understanding, more love; truly, heaven on earth.

Even when challenges arise, seeing the illusionary nature of reality eases the challenge. You *see* that it is just made up in the moment. Observe the thought, don't examine—let the pure power of thought flow, and the reality will change. We hold heaven in our hands; we hold the answer in our soul.

CHAPTER 19
ISLAND LIVING

Island living is a wonderful gift that my husband and I appreciate more each day. It offers a quiet, slow paced environment, and respite from a busy world, if you're open to it. Not everyone likes it; you either fall in love with the small community lifestyle and ambiance that make up our island, or you don't.

We decided to take in the sunset last night at Vesuvius Beach. As the sun lowered behind the mountains in the distance, we viewed the ocean before us, with several sailboats anchored in the harbor, suffused in a golden light. Silhouetted against this amazing light was a wooden dock coming from a seaside home, reaching far into the ocean. The dock had metal hand rails standing on each side, all shining as if made from freshly spun gold. It seemed to disappear into nothingness. It was breathtaking; we observed this scene with wonder. It was like a pathway to infinity.

My husband commented that we are living in the banner of our website—the photo of the banner was taken by Ken—and those words struck me, reminding me how lucky we are to be living in a community relatively free of crime, where neighbors are always available and more than willing to come to each other's assistance, no questions asked other than "How can we help?"

It takes some folks time to appreciate the limits of an island; the fact that you can't leave and return any time you want—the first ferry is at 6 a.m. and the last ferry back to the island from the city is at 9 p.m. But we love it.

As we drove home, we continued our journey past our turnoff, to see what was happening in the village. Winding our way toward our destination, we observed how quiet the roads were, and that the grocery store parking lot was pretty much deserted, as were the only

Chinese restaurant and the Pizza place. Stillness pervaded until we reached the core of our wee village, a beautiful setting, overlooking the harbor.

There was music playing at the Tree House Restaurant, and people sitting at small table groupings, enjoying chatting with each other and listening to the band. We parked and listened for a while, then headed home, content and with smiles on our faces, thinking how lucky we were to be living on this beautiful island.

Earlier that day we had noticed three quaintly decorated pianos situated in various locations along the village streets. Curious about this unusual display, we then read in our local newspaper, *Gulf Islands Driftwood*, "Mysterious street pianos captivate Salt Spring Island crowds." A resident was quoted as saying, "Puts a lot of joy into your day," as she played an inspired rendition of *Bridge Over Troubled Waters*. What a brilliant idea!

We feel like we have *island living* in our minds, mostly quiet and peaceful, with the occasional music playing, magical sunsets and inspired ideas to enjoy, all blending together in harmony, providing interest and wonder, as well as comfort and protection from a busy mind.

We all have *island living* in our hearts and souls, whether we live on an island or not. Such is the extraordinary capacity of the human spirit. We are very, very grateful.

Chapter 20
Light at the End of the Tunnel

A s I was going through my picture gallery the other day, a particular photo of the "light at the end of the tunnel" brought a smile to my face. I took this photo in a medieval town, called Seguret, in Provence, near the villa our family had rented for our vacation.

Early one Sunday morning, we strolled down the country road to explore the village. When we entered the enormous arched gateway into the community, it was as if we had stepped back in time. No residents were visible, no coffee shops were open, no tourists; we felt as if we were in an enchanted hamlet.

As we continued wandering about, we spotted a narrow side street with the sun glowing at the end. The ancient homes seemed to lean toward one another overhead, and with tree branches creating shadows, we felt as if we were enclosed in an arbor of greenery. We were captivated by the mystical charm, and stood in silent admiration.

The inviting light at the end of the path illustrated what I was feeling. Finally, I was listening to the voice inside and *seeing* the light.

Previously, I had over-committed to my work opportunities and could feel I wasn't as present as I know I can be. My spirit had been flagging as I kept piling more and more form on my invisible, but feel-able, energy. I love being in service so it was very difficult to take time for myself, to pause and reflect.

The inner voice persisted, and as I began to pace myself with more common sense, my spirits lifted; I felt much calmer, and clarity emerged. As my spirit lightened, I even felt gleeful at postponing opportunities to be in service to others. I know this may sound selfish—but bear with me. For the first time in quite a while, I was tuned into being in service to my True Self.

Completing my last Skype session with a client, a wonderful

conversation about how practical and natural wisdom is, I felt that inner light re-ignite, and insight occurred.

I realized that the tunnel was my little mind keeping me busy, captivated by the form of life. The big Mind is the light, shining through the form, illuminating a pathway to follow. Big Mind and little mind are One, so there is perfect symmetry; illustrating that form and formless are One—pure energy.

Sometimes we may think pure energy needs no nourishment; and in fact, it doesn't. However, our bodies are physical form and do need rest. Our minds also need space for reflection and for wisdom to come through. When we respect the form and the formless, somehow this respect seems to lessen the gap between what is and what isn't. And we begin to live more fully in what is.

Chapter 21
Home is Wherever You Are

As tiredness evaporates in the mists of time, stillness emerges. Only now is present; not yesterday, not tomorrow, only now. Stillness offers space for insight to occur, when one is ready.

Reclining comfortably on the beach lounge in Mexico, protected from the sun by palm trees overhead, a feeling of gratitude swept over me. I felt like I was in the perfect place in the universe, in this moment of time. Utter contentment filled my soul. Glancing over at my husband, we exchanged a smile, and then drifted into our own solitude.

It occurred to me that wherever I go, most of the time I feel at home, whether in my garden, office, driving on the highway or on vacation in Mexico. I felt more deeply the truth that home is inside that stillness, inside our own psyche, in that connection with spiritual essence.

The feeling brought to mind how different it was in the early days of my mental evolution, when I didn't feel at home anywhere. In those days, I was so insecure that I was scared to drive on the ferry to visit Syd Banks on Salt Spring. I was scared to fly, to travel on my own, to go anywhere on my own. I needed to have Ken by my side or I stayed home.

How can someone change so much? I didn't think an ordinary person could change their whole personality. Certainly, I had seen the transformation in Syd after his epiphany, but I felt that was due to the Enlightenment he'd experienced.

And yet Syd was a simple, ordinary working man who had an extraordinary experience. He remained down to earth afterwards, although the feeling that emanated from him, as he shared the mystery he'd realized, was not of this world. To me, his words and that feeling seemed beyond the ken of ordinary mortals.

Not so to Syd. He continued to coach those he mentored to embrace being ordinary, telling us that in being ordinary, we'd find out we were extraordinary.

It was puzzling and I never believed it was possible until it happened to me. When I began to dip my toe into the water of true knowledge, I gained strength, confidence, and a willingness to be scared and still move forward.

What I discovered was that, as I moved forward, all my anxious thoughts began to vanish. I began to see that being static can promote distress. Moving forward slowed the thought cycle of fear enough to let in a sense of assurance that I could do more on my own than I had given myself credit for. The feeling of self-reliance was intoxicating and gave me more courage to continue my inner journey.

The sound of waves brought me back into the present as they rolled onto shore, blending in perfect harmony with the whisper of the palm fronds, swaying gently in the breeze. The rays of sunlight coming through the palms and the birds chirping overhead entranced me, and continued to soothe my mind. The heat of the sun eased my bones till I felt like I was melting into the lounge. Indeed, home is wherever we are.

CHAPTER 22
LEARNING HOW TO SHARE

It's an interesting situation, when sharing what you think you know can innocently act as a barrier to learning something new.

My initial resistance to what Syd was sharing about the Three Principles continued for well over a year. Finally, when I felt I had come to the end of my rope, I had a totally unexpected insight about thought that transformed my life.

Syd encouraged me, as well as some of his other students, to talk about what we were learning with people who came to the regular Friday evening gatherings on Salt Spring Island. He let us know how important it was to share our insights. *"When you share true knowledge, you release that deep feeling. Have you any idea how powerful that is?"*

Well of course, we really didn't. But we did the best we could, and there were times when we got a glimmer of the power.

As time went on, mental health professionals began coming to the gatherings on the island. Syd would talk with the audience, and although there were times when one of us might feel inspired to share, often times the deep feeling coming from Syd pervaded the room and would have the whole audience spellbound and wordless.

It wasn't too long after the Friday evening gatherings that two psychologists, Drs. Roger Mills and George Pransky, invited Syd to the United States to speak at a university in Oregon. Syd invited me to accompany him, and one of the first things he taught me was to share what I had realized about thought.

When he saw how anxious I was about speaking with the audience, Syd quietly said, *"Just share what you know and you'll be fine, dearie."*

I found that statement to be absolutely true. Yes, I blathered on stage for the first five minutes, but then, as if by magic, I slipped past my insecurity and went home where insights are born; that state of consciousness that resides within each and every soul.

I felt so at peace, as if I were being held and guided by essence. Words poured out without thought, effortlessly. Time stood still. And then it was finished. I felt like I came back to the world of form. I scanned the audience, noticing the stillness in the room. And I knew for the first time: the power of the deep feeling Syd spoke about will manifest, when we get out of the way.

And so it went for some time. Then, as I became more comfortable in my knowledge, my ego began to be seduced by what I knew. Whenever Syd would talk, I would think to myself, "Oh yes, I get that. I know what he's talking about." And I would share this with him. Consequently, I stopped learning. . .I already knew. . .

I noticed that my sharing didn't have the same feeling or impact on the people or groups I was working with, but I attributed that to "They're just not getting it. They're just not ready."

Syd never directly said anything to me about this. He would look at me with a certain glint in his eye, but he refrained from calling me to task. He let me know that true knowledge is infinite. "*We never come to the end of our learning, Elsie. We have the pleasure and enjoyment of being lifelong students, which keeps us humble, vital and alive.*" I nodded my head in agreement.

Syd simply stopped talking to me about the true nature of life, of the Principles, and so on, whenever I glided into "Yes, I know that." His silence spoke louder than words. I began to feel something was amiss. My mind stilled, and finally, finally, my consciousness informed me I didn't know as much as I thought I did. The door to new learning opened. My inner journey was reignited and evolution continued.

Such is the awesome power of our inner "coach" coupled with the gentle touch of a true Master coach.

Chapter 23
Seeing Life as a Child

As I connect more deeply with my true nature, I find my life is simpler; feelings are more childlike, more in the moment. I enjoy life as is—whatever is happening in the moment, just is. I view life with more innocence, with less blame than I used to have, less judgment of myself or others. I don't think as much about things as I used to. I just live life without much extraneous thought.

It's not that I don't have questions about life, about work, relationships, or whatever; but I trust the answers will come—and they do, from inside-out. There's ease in living like this.

When my husband was seriously ill recently, our wisdom walked by our side, shoulder to shoulder, it seemed. The feeling was very comforting, offering solace. I know wisdom is inside; I'm just offering a description of how wisdom felt during that medically challenging time. Our faith was childlike; trust was present, assuring us that all would be well, even when we weren't certain that it would be. . .

Another example occurred while visiting friends in Brighton, England. Prior to an evening talk my colleagues had arranged, I went for a walk to quiet my mind. The field behind my friends' home was a mass of red poppies, strikingly beautiful. I wandered through the meadow on a well-trodden path and came to another pasture, where several horses were standing together, very still. I stopped in front of the animals, silently appraising them. I couldn't get over how motionless they were. I'd never seen anything like it and was absolutely fascinated. I stood mesmerized by their stillness, and then reached down to pull up some dried grass to feed one through the wire fence. I felt deeply moved by this silent communication, and thought how all things in life truly are the same energy.

I turned back on the path through the poppy field and felt

compelled to lie down on my back and contemplate the sky. I drank in the beauty until a thought crossed my mind; if someone came walking by, they'd wonder what on earth was going on, seeing an older woman flat on her back, gazing at the heavens. With a smile on my face, I got up and found my way home. As I walked, I had to chuckle. In my late 60's, I felt like a child again and I loved it. I felt at one with nature, I felt a synergy with the animals, with the land. I felt I had bathed in the essence of life. It was a privilege.

CHAPTER 24
SEEING OUR HUMAN FRAILTIES WITH GENTLENESS

For several years now, my primary focus has been on the spiritual nature of the Principles, of humanity, and of life. This was the direction the late Sydney Banks pointed toward, in his sharing with me and with all his students. He said we would find the answer to the world's dilemmas, including our own, when we considered more deeply the formless source of reality.

The passion and certainty with which he expressed this moved me; it touched the core of my being. As I began to reflect on the true nature of our world, I experienced a shift in my perspective. I found a deeper sense of the spiritual nature of the Principles, as well as more understanding of the practical aspects of my everyday life.

Gentleness began to permeate my world. I didn't take life so seriously, nor judge myself or others with as much gusto. Things that used to appall or dismay lost their sting. For example, if I felt that Syd's work was being trivialized or commercialized, I saw that everything has its purpose in the world; that life gives us assignments to help us *see* the illusion.

I saw that people are so wise, so discerning, that they would recognize truth when they felt it, because they *are* it. I saw that no one could hurt or damage the Principles. How can you damage the formless energy of all things? It's beyond the human capacity to do this.

Appreciation for universal order and guidance began to emerge in my vision. This appreciation cleared the deck for compassion, for *seeing* our human frailties with gentleness. I began to connect our human nature more closely with our spiritual nature, seeing the Oneness of the form and the formless. We are, indeed, a vessel for the spiritual essence and as such, it serves us well to acknowledge the human part of us with respect, patience, and love.

CHAPTER 25
OUR BEST FRIEND—WISDOM

Wisdom is always available, beneath the surface of our thinking, if we can still our mind enough to listen.

Oftentimes, even when our mind is not still, wisdom has a knack of making itself heard, refusing to give up, continuing to knock on our door. Because that's who we are, that's what our true nature is; wise, clear, our best friend.

The two most essential factors in honoring our best friend: know we are the Principles in motion, that it's unnecessary to "apply" the Principles to our life. They *are* our life. We may lose sight of that from time to time; however, that doesn't negate the spiritual truth that we are what we seek.

There is such relief in discontinuing our search for a better, easier life. We already have it—inside. We're sitting on a pot of gold. Actually, we are the pot of gold! Embrace it, respect it, and it will serve you forever, providing a life imbued with understanding and contentment.

The second factor is realizing the full power of the feeling of well-being. Know that the feeling is the vehicle for change. That deep feeling provides a pathway to insights which further our inner journey. Insights come from our innate wisdom, Mind in motion. Nothing to do—just be open to that spiritual fact.

"*Don't try and figure it out; just get the feeling.*" How often have we heard Sydney Banks make that statement? From the beginning of his teaching, that was a constant refrain: "*Just get the feeling and the information you seek will come to you.*"

I used to puzzle over this. In my mind, this counsel was far too simple. I felt I needed to voice my problems, and work on them to find solution. How could a feeling bring resolution?

Yet to my surprise and delight, I learned from experience that this was true. The less I thought about my problems, the more relaxed and at peace I felt. Understanding and resolution seemed to appear out of nowhere. The *feeling* releases wisdom. How about that! Nothing to do—just live in the feeling the best we can, and our life will continue to blossom.

I've been a student of the Three Principles for over four decades and I can honestly say that the Principles take us to the essence of our being, which is expressed by a feeling of resonance; that *feeling* is the bridge to our true nature.

CHAPTER 26
TRUST WISDOM "BUT". . .

I'd like to share a story, following on the theme of the previous chapter. I love when a client asks a question that concerns them and in responding to their query, without knowing the answer prior to my reply, the words slip out in a way that helps both of us see more. When the recipient is touched by the truth of the response, it's a win-win situation. I love the mutually beneficial learning!

A young man, Eli, reached out to me with this question: "I am encountering some confusion over what is meant for one to 'follow their wisdom.' I have been involved with the Three Principles understanding for just over two years now, and have seen incredible and beautiful transformations in myself and others. The work carried out by you and others in the community fills me with so much hope and love; I can't help starting this message off by expressing my gratitude for this understanding.

"As a Three Principles practitioner, I am currently working with others in the community to share and deepen my understanding, and am enrolled in training to assist me in my journey. I see that we all have access to our innate wellbeing and wisdom when the thinking mind quiets, and that in those moments we can be 'guided;' however, the message I am hearing from some is, 'Following wisdom is useful, but it doesn't hurt to have a plan.' To me, this comes across as 'It's OK to follow your wisdom, but. . .'

"My question is: as one looks further and further in the direction of the quiet space where wisdom resides, are we not effectively surrendering to wisdom, and allowing ourselves to be carried by it? I feel as if the message being shared could be holding us back from falling deeper and deeper into the space within."

This was my reply: "I'm touched by your wisdom, Eli. You see clearly that wisdom is our birthright so of course it makes sense to listen to it.

"In response to your question about trusting wisdom, yet hearing some say 'but it doesn't hurt to have a plan,' I know what you mean. It's a slippery slope. On one hand, our spiritual nature/wisdom is the 'master.' What I've experienced is, the more I trust that internal wisdom fully, the more it guides me. Opportunities seem to appear out of the blue, and things just fall into place. I love seeing the plan Universal Mind has for us to evolve and unfold in a way that is unique to each individual.

"Having said that, I have, at times, made a plan from my intellect. Sometimes it works; other times Universal Mind has other plans. For me, this is life's assignment, to see what we see; to listen to our wisdom more fully and see how the intellect and wisdom can work together in harmony.

"I call the learning that occurs when this happens 'continuing education.' The intellect comes from Universal Mind and takes shape in human form. That's the game of life; formless/form. Universal Mind/little mind. Both are the same Mind used in two different ways; wisdom and personal thinking. Different sides of the same coin.

"The beauty of this partnership, as I see it, is that Mind/wisdom is the master and personal intellect is in service to wisdom. When we listen to our wisdom, our intellectual potential is enhanced and works to our benefit. This is the space inside, our spiritual inheritance, the wisdom that we slip into which guides us.

"When we don't listen to wisdom, we may have to wander around a bit to find our way back 'home.' What's reassuring during this journey is that we're always at 'home,' even when we may lose our way from time to time.

"I hope this is helpful, Eli. The main thing is to trust your own inner knowing and be assured that will serve as an example to others, simply by you living in your wisdom."

Eli replied, "A lot of what I 'know' is being left behind and life is calling for me to step up. In light of this I reflect on your words and follow the pointing of my heart."

Chapter 27
The Power and Relevance of Sydney Bank's Story

During my business travels recently to the UK and Europe, I had the privilege of sharing my understanding of the Three Principles that Syd uncovered over forty years ago.

Everyone I spoke to and at every presentation I gave, people were drawn to Syd's story, as well as the message of hope and transformation that the Principles offer. Some in the audience were unfamiliar with Syd's story; others had heard a bit.

The feeling that manifested in the room while sharing the fact of Syd's spontaneous epiphany stilled the intellect of the audience, and they were clearly moved by the miracle that happened to him, despite some puzzlement.

I related my own story as well; about my strong resistance to Syd's message of how we create our experience in life, and how, despite my intellectual struggle, I had a moment of insight that moved me to a new understanding of how the mind works. This understanding opened a whole new world for me, filled with peace of mind and contentment such as I'd never experienced before.

I shared all this in three different venues, two different countries, each with diverse audiences with varied degrees of understanding; some new to the Principles, others very well grounded, and everywhere in between.

Common ground was established, despite the complete diversity of the audiences, via Syd's story and how the Principles lead us to our true nature. Within a very short time, the *feeling* of our true nature, united in the moment, expressed itself in the venue. The feeling was undeniable, and as I mentioned earlier in the chapter, stilled the intellect of everyone present. Even when a few individuals in the audience thought they weren't "getting it," they were moved by the feeling and remained in the room.

During the break, I had the opportunity to speak with one who felt this way, and shared my observation that despite his intellect telling him he wasn't "getting it," he was still with us. Therefore his wisdom was holding him in place. His whole being lit up at this statement; the simplicity and power of truth kept him still, even though his mind was racing. He remained in the room, enjoying the feeling, even though he believed he didn't understand the Principles.

This fills me with wonder; that we don't have to understand the Principles in order to *feel* them and benefit. When we feel them, this means we have a degree of knowing—not belief—but *knowing*.

The deep feeling that filled the room at each venue allowed learning to emerge with such ease that people were unaware they were learning. They were just *feeling* at peace, which is the groundwork for insight, either in the moment or later on. It doesn't really matter. Just the feeling is relevant. When that feeling is present, the work is being done, spiritually.

One participant had this to say: "Profound is the word that best summarizes just what a shift I have experienced. I found the gentle, spiritual space that you held for us allowed my whole mind to clear, slow down and then hear things afresh. I do really believe that I will not only be able to serve myself with much greater grace and health but I will be able to share the understanding with others with much greater clarity and simplicity and knowing. My heartfelt thanks to you for sharing your truth with so much love and gentleness......it has touched my heart."

This is how Syd taught us, the early pioneers and all who came along during the many years of Syd's teaching. He taught us by the feeling; he helped us see that information is contained within that feeling. That feeling is wisdom speaking to us, quietly revealing who and what we really are.

Syd's transformation was the first example of these spiritual, formless Principles giving us the power to create form; the form of experience. When he realized "*Insecurity is thought,*" his personality and behavior changed completely. Although I became increasingly troubled by the change in Syd, it also intrigued me, and despite myself, I found it hopeful.

After Syd's experience, he walked in a different world; a seemingly mystical world that I didn't understand. However, I liked the feeling. His transformation, coupled with the feeling he lived in, kept me close, till I had my own insight that started my journey.

Such is the power of Syd's story and why I place such importance on sharing it. Let us never lose sight of this—Syd's story is truth manifest in the world today, letting us know we have the Principles within us, a gift for humans to make form. Together, let's help keep his legacy alive.

CHAPTER 28
CAN PEOPLE CHANGE?

Can people change? And if they can, is change sustainable? Before I knew about the transformative power of the Three Principles, I thought people had a fixed personality. In my limited observations, I never saw anyone's personality change, permanently, until I witnessed the transformation in Sydney Banks after his epiphany.

Even when I observed the change in his personality and in his behavior, I didn't trust that it was sustainable. I waited for the other shoe to drop—sooner or later, I felt he would revert back to his old patterns of insecurity.

His enjoyment of the simple pleasures of life and the love he bestowed on his family continued to blossom, the whole time I knew him. This behavior was not typical of Syd before he realized that insecurity was thought. Although he'd always been a kind husband and father, feelings of insecurity had diminished his enjoyment of life and family. The sustained change in his behavior was a powerful beacon to me, despite my intellectual resistance to the information he shared about his discovery.

My skepticism was so strong in the early days that at one point, when Syd arrived at our home for a visit and I asked him what he'd been up to, the story he told me sounded far-fetched, to say the least. He showed me a flyer announcing the talk he'd given at a major university to the departments of psychology and psychiatry. My face reflected my disbelief. I found this so unbelievable that I thought he'd gone to a quick-print shop to have this flyer made up, just to fool me.

My cynicism prevented me from seeing the black and white evidence of Syd's presentation printed in the flyer. You know that old saying "Seeing is believing"? I saw the flyer but I still didn't believe.

Thought creates reality. This is a spiritual fact. My thoughts created a barrier to seeing what was before my very eyes. And yet, my inner core was stirring, disturbing my intellect, making me question the very foundation of my belief system. How could an ex-welder talk to a group of mental health professionals? At a university, no less? Why was he invited? What could he possibly talk about? Why was he happier than he was before? How was he able to enjoy life like he did now, when he didn't before?

What I love about this story is that it shows how our innate wisdom is always at work, despite doubt or resistance. Our True Self is awake and ready to be heard. It only waits for us to be ready to hear. What more can we ask?

CHAPTER 29
WISHFUL THINKING VERSUS WISDOM

In the early days of my learning, I struggled with trying to comprehend Syd when he talked about how we use thought to create our reality. I couldn't fathom his logic. I would argue that I used thought in a positive manner, telling him how diligently I wished for a more harmonious relationship with my husband and children, how I wished for a lot of things. I let him know that I prayed to be a better person, with more understanding of others, and to have less anger and judgment.

To my dismay, my wishful thinking and prayers didn't produce results. This type of thinking actually kept me in a dismissive state of mind. No results meant that my positive thinking didn't work. Therefore, my usage of thought had nothing to do with my experience of reality. Consequently, I felt that Syd didn't know what he was talking about. . . yet I couldn't end my relationship with him.

The one thing that kept me intrigued was the feeling Syd lived in. That feeling warmed my heart and soul. Syd's feeling of well-being kept me near, despite my intellectual resistance. I've always attributed the feeling I had then to Syd's presence.

Ultimately, I became aware that even then, it was my own wisdom manifesting via my feeling of well-being. Of course, Syd was a catalyst, but it was my own feeling of happiness I was experiencing. That feeling prompted some change in my behavior, despite my lack of understanding. I became kinder and less judgmental, to myself and to my family and friends.

Wisdom was changing me, naturally and without wishful thinking. The *feeling* was teaching me, evolving me. The feeling stilled my busy mind so I could *hear* my wisdom.

Wisdom came forth as a result of an elevation in my level of consciousness so subtle, so natural, that I was unaware at the time that I'd had a shift. Only recently did I realize, almost four decades later, that the feeling was already changing me, even before I had my first insight.

I'd always thought my first insight about thought creating feeling was what had advanced me. And it did—coupled with the fact that I had already been embracing the feeling of well-being more of the time.

Wishful thinking comes from the intellect and doesn't promote change. True change is initiated by insight, new thought from Mind. Consciousness is awareness of this new thought which produces a shift in understanding. Thought is the bridge between formless and form. Three Principles working in unison, bringing about spiritual and mental evolution, are how progression takes place naturally, from within.

CHAPTER 30
TIED TO GUILT

Do you ever find yourself hesitant to make a decision because you don't want to hurt someone's feelings? Do you ruminate over this lack of decisiveness, giving yourself reason after reason why you can't do what you really would like to do? Do you ever go along with someone, and then berate yourself because you really didn't want to do it and it doesn't feel good? I would answer "yes" to every one of the above questions. . . and I don't think I'm in the minority.

The more I learn from wisdom, the more often I find a way to navigate through these situations. Following the *feeling* is the best guide. Patience is the partner of feeling. With these two qualities residing within us, it's nearly impossible to go off track, but we do.

For example, this past year has been the busiest work time for me, ever. I decided to take the summer off, with wisdom and my husband encouraging me. I thought it would be easy. However, what I didn't realize is how tied I was to being in service. Saying "no" to requests from clients, prospective clients, and friends for coaching, catch-up calls, and various other needs was very difficult. I harbored many thoughts about being selfish, inconsiderate, and a host of other dark thoughts in the middle of the night.

One day, as I slipped away from my busy schedule and treated myself to a morning walk, it occurred to me that I was tied to guilt. Guilty thoughts filled my consciousness and of course, because we are the creator of our feelings, the feeling of guilt was prominent in my experience. All of a sudden, I realized it had been a long time since I'd taken time to go for a walk. That shift was the beginning of new thoughts starting to flow and guilt starting to evaporate. I saw the logic of once again embracing a deeper level of wisdom, allowing space in my mind for insights to flourish, and creativity to unfold.

With more "leg room" in my mind, patience emerged. I didn't feel rushed to do anything. Where was the hurry that I had been experiencing? Hurry is tied to guilt. Hurry to finish a project, hurry to finish a call, looking at the calendar to see what was next on the agenda. Nonsense! All made up by my thinking.

Gentleness began to fill my heart, understanding for myself and for others. While I had been in a rushed state of mind, I debated on how best to tell my clients I was easing up on my work load. Previously, my reasons were apologetic and defensive. With patience coming into play, my ability to communicate was diplomatic. I simply and naturally let people know I was unavailable until the autumn, or referred them to other practitioners. Some decided to wait (I had been curious if they would). Many applauded my taking the time off and wished me well. Others shared that they had realized they could take more time for themselves as well. Being true to mySELF provided an example.

It feels so good to thank our own wisdom when it grasps our hand and pulls us from an old habit we've slipped into. It may be over-thinking, over-eating, over-drinking, over-judging...or whatever it is that, when noticed by wisdom, provides an opportunity to learn and grow. Wisdom dissolves guilt. How wonderful is that?!

It's our world, our experience, that we create. Why not create an experience that nourishes the soul. When we do this, the spiritual energy that we are all part of resonates and sends an enriching ripple out into the world, helping others find the spiritual logic that's so important to inner evolution. The way it looks to me, this is the best, most profound way of *being* in service—without being tied to service.

It honors that mystical saying of Syd's, *"Doing without doing."*

CHAPTER 31
PERSPECTIVE ON DEPRESSION

First of all, I want to be clear that I am a layperson sharing my thoughts on depression. In no way do I want to minimize the crippling strength of despairing thoughts that have the power to incapacitate an individual as well as create angst amongst those closest to them.

Seeing how clients' depression has been alleviated once they came to an understanding of the power humans have to create our own experience has inspired me to write this chapter, as well as seeing my own depression simply fade from my world.

Before I was introduced to the Three Principles, there was a period in my life when I was a young wife and mother of two children, and felt caught up in utter despair. "Is this all there is? What is the point of going on?" were consistent refrains in my mind.

I felt trapped by my marriage and by my family, with no place to turn. I tried to self-medicate with alcohol but my misery increased. My only solace was sleep, when the kids were in school, and even that was disturbed by my busy, frantic mind grappling with my dilemmas.

I contemplated suicide and found myself alone driving in the car at 100 mph, ready to turn the wheel and fly into space off the crest of a hill. At the last moment, I couldn't do it. I slowed down and came back to earth with a thump, sobbing my heart out that I didn't have the courage to leave this world. You may say that's not depression. Perhaps not; I'm just sharing what my experience felt like to me.

Thoughts of what would happen to my children and husband provided a thin thread of light and prevented me from ending my life. Thoughts equal the quality of reality. Many years later, I connected those thoughts of my family as the thoughts that gave me a tenuous, but precious hold on life. At that moment, so long after my mental anguish, I realized more fully how powerful we are; how we hold the answer to life's questions in the palm of our hand, in the depths of our soul.

I also want to share my observations of other people who had been diagnosed with depression, whom I've met over the many years of being a student of the Principles. In the early days, when Sydney Banks' work was first being discovered by people on Salt Spring Island, where he lived, many came down his driveway, lost in the mire of their thinking and without hope.

Over a cup of tea, and with some words of wisdom from Syd, their innate mental health rose to the surface, as bubbles deep in the ocean naturally rise to the top of the sea. People left his presence imbued with strength and faith that they too were whole and healthy at their core.

Seeing these transformations time and again unquestionably inspired me and countless others, including the mental health professionals who were drawn to the island. They had heard rumors of an ordinary working man who had been blessed with a simple, profound insight, resulting in the extraordinary power to help people find solace in their lives. We are all blessed with the potential to offer hope and peace of mind.

One of my own examples is of a woman who came to a training I did in Tampa, Florida. I clearly recall how she was so moved by her insight about innate mental health, she intuitively felt she could decrease her psychotropic medication, with her doctor's reluctant approval. Shortly after that, she and her psychiatrist agreed she no longer needed to continue her therapy, but that she would come in should the need arise.

Sounds far-fetched? At the time, when this woman told me the story of decreasing her meds the day after attending my training, I certainly thought she was stretching it a bit. To this day, twenty years later, she is still functioning from a state of well-being. She started her own business and is an outstanding teacher of the Principles, sharing her wisdom and inspiring others who are caught up in the trap of their faulty thinking.

Countless stories abound of people finding their way to mental health, once they realize who and what they are, on the inside. Their thoughts of despair at this point lack the power to stick. At the very least, the thoughts lack the power to remain permanently in charge.

Three Principles psychiatrists have told me that medication can ease the mental pain and help slow an individual's thinking enough so they can *hear* their inner wisdom and gain insight. They submit that in addition to hearing wisdom, learning that they have the power to think and create is the ultimate solution. I concur: trust that your wisdom will guide you to your innate mental health. Wisdom *is* your innate health.

Some medical experts talk about depression being a "brain disease." Again, I'm no expert but I've seen that when people who have struggled with depression, myself included, understand there are Principles underlying the human experience, and that Thought creates feeling, that understanding relieves the depression. Therefore it seems logical to me that there is a deeper source, beyond the brain, that contributes to the health and chemistry of the brain.

Here is the crux of the matter. When thoughts change, so do feelings. It follows that when depressive thoughts alter, so do the depressing feelings and corresponding behavior. My feelings and behavior stabilized as my thoughts changed to hopeful thoughts.

This is also what I observed in others. As soon as they realized the correlation between thought and feeling, their default setting of mental health kicked in automatically, over-riding their faulty thinking. The result was peace, well-being, and contentment.

Mental health is not found through will-power. This natural resource already exists within us all. Simply realizing this spiritual fact and embracing it brings our spiritual power to life, and changes the form of our world. Another way of saying this is: Consciousness is hope and transformation in action.

CHAPTER 32
GOING DEEPER INTO OUR TRUE NATURE

Sometimes when students/clients are encouraged to "go deeper," they may feel their grounding is not good enough. On the contrary! Wherever someone is in their learning is exactly where they are supposed to be. They've already laid the ground work or foundation for the next step of continuing education, a lifelong, enriching journey.

This came to light in some mentoring conversations I had with a young practitioner, Jon, who wanted to deepen his understanding, both for his own learning and to better serve his clients. Our conversations deepened naturally, simply by my listening to him, drawing out and reinforcing his wisdom.

I was curious about how Jon worked with his clients and asked him to give me the flavor of how he talked with them. The success he was having was very good, but as we conversed, it became apparent there were areas where Jon could help his clients connect the dots more.

In other words, Jon could help his clients see that the outcomes they were experiencing were a result of the fact that their personal thinking was slowing down. Because of this fact, they were more relaxed; therefore more clarity and common sense were emerging, guiding them in their everyday living. They were automatically using the Principles in the way they are meant to be used—with wisdom.

As I talked with Jon, he confessed that until that moment, he hadn't realized why he himself was feeling more relaxed and content in his life, or where his own success was coming from. He'd just taken the change for granted, and hadn't connected the dots back to living more fully in his true nature.

Further education, highlighting the role of Consciousness, proved insightful to my client, and he was then able to share this

ELSIE SPITTLE

with his clients. Jon simply hadn't realized that when positive change occurs, it's very important to not only acknowledge it, but to help those you serve see where it comes from; to be aware that accessing your inner wisdom, your true nature, is the Principles in action. It may seem obvious to some, but believe me, what is obvious to one is not necessarily obvious to another.

It was an eye-opening conversation, not only for the young practitioner, but for me as well. It reminded me that I often slip into taking my life for granted. This is one of the reasons I love being in service, as best I can. The learning potential is always available and is such an enriching and enlightening experience. There are few things better in the world than to help someone discover their inner core.

The next mentoring conversation with this young man brought more insights. Jon started off by sharing how much he'd seen old habits come into play that had never been visible before. He was feeling a little chagrined that his ego had been so prominent and had hidden his old habits so effectively. He said that when he first started to notice the old patterns, his blamed himself for not doing better and his ego came into play with judgment. His personal thinking temporarily hijacked his wisdom.

What I *heard* was that his awareness, his true nature, was more engaged, which showed up his old thinking patterns, thus allowing him to move past them. I thought it was excellent progress and pointed this out to him. He thought it was ego.

A deep silence occurred; a moment of reflection, then his face lit up as if the light had been turned on, and indeed it had. The dots had been connected and he was home, inside where all the answers lie. I could *feel* him resonating with the rich feeling of our engagement. I knew he was ready to serve more deeply.

CHAPTER 33
GOING DEEPER INTO MIND

Universal Mind will take care of moving us along, by prompting us when the time is right. The more I trust this spiritual process, the knowledge that wisdom is working in complete accord within me, even when I think it's not, the more balanced my life becomes. I've always been keen on seeing the practical side of life as well as the profound. I need to be touched by the logic, by the results of insight, to have a clear *knowing*.

Let me give you an example. As I've mentioned before, it took me well over a year before the understanding Syd was sharing with me made sense via an insight; *my* insight, not Syd sharing his insights.

The insight I had was an expression of my true nature. It not only moved me past my anger and resistance—that insight provided me with the proof and logic of how my thoughts create my feelings.

What was so powerful for me was to be free, in that moment of insight, of my feelings of fear and frustration, which I had always attributed to external circumstances. The fact that in a split second, I was no longer feeling anger—when a moment before I'd been consumed with rage—was proof that a change of thought can instantly change one's experience. From that moment on there was no looking back.

To this day, I continue to learn from my wisdom, sometimes with complete openness, and other times a bit reluctantly. Reluctantly, because I may have decided on a path for my work and then I'll get an email or call from a prospective client who does not fit that path of how I feel my work should unfold. Does this sound familiar?

I'll give you an example. After taking time off this summer, I came to the conclusion that I wanted to mentor practitioners; that was my path. I didn't want to do personal development anymore. I felt I'd been there and done that. While I loved serving in that capacity, I felt it was time to move on.

However, after receiving several requests that didn't fit my supposed path but touched my heart, I knew wisdom was knocking on my door once again; I opened the door. To say I've learned so much and been moved to greater depths of understanding by honoring these requests barely gives credit to the power of listening to the *feeling* within.

We may have a path or a goal in mind. Universal Mind *sees* the big picture and It requires us to forget our personal self and forge ahead into our True Self. It's up to us to say, "How can I serve?" rather than "I will serve this way." This truly is going deeper into our true nature, deeper into Mind.

CHAPTER 34
SOUL TO SOUL

As I began my journey learning about the Three Principles, my True Self became more visible. This resulted in my becoming more independent. Previously, in my insecure state of mind, I'd always relied on someone else—my father, my husband, anyone I considered more secure than I.

Finding my inner being gave me more confidence and I soon started to venture out into the world more. The first time Sydney Banks asked me to talk at one of the local gatherings on Salt Spring, I was almost frozen with fear. I managed to say a few words regarding what I was learning about thought and then sat for the rest of the evening, wondering if it had been good enough, if people had gotten anything from my sharing, and so on; lots of anxious thinking.

Eventually, I discovered that the more I shared from my heart, the less nervous I felt. It was as if the gift of sharing opened the door to my soul. As my soul took center stage, I felt like I'd gone *home* and the feeling of love permeated the room. The audience was touched and their souls responded; the gathering was soul to soul rather than personality to personality.

In my personal relationship with Ken, I discovered that as I became more engaged with my wisdom, my independence flourished. Although it took him a bit of time to adjust, Ken liked the new woman in his life. Our conversations were far more interesting, as we talked about everyday matters and also shared what we were learning about ourselves. We respected each other's opinion and listened to one another in a way that we never had before. I found this way of communicating exciting. It added vitality to our relationship.

It was fascinating to notice that as I gained confidence and independence, I saw Ken with new eyes, as he was seeing me. We also were seeing each other soul to soul rather than personality to personality.

This way of *seeing* lends itself to feeling proud of the advances your partner/family/friends make in life. *Seeing* eliminates ego from one's relationships and promotes harmony. Ego stimulates disharmony.

In my earlier insecurity, I used to feel envy or jealousy if someone close to me got wonderful opportunities or went on a special vacation. I'd think, why them? Why not me? Now I'm thrilled when something good happens for someone. It feels like it's happening for me too! It speaks to connection; that we're all linked at a spiritual level, soul to soul.

My work also changed as I focused more on connection and less on personality. I began to see that when I talked to clients as "soul to soul," the feeling that was evoked bypassed their thinking. This deep feeling connected directly to the invisible core of our spiritual nature.

Rather than speaking to what was being presented by the client— behavioral issues at the thinking, form level— engaging at the soul level resulted in far more impact, helping clients touch their own wisdom and gain insight.

This is connecting at Principle, the formless energy level where all the answers we seek are found. This connection offers a natural ease and freedom in living more fully in our spiritual residence.

Chapter 35
The Joy of Learning

Aconversation with a dear friend brought about some fresh awareness. Jeanie was telling me about a new hobby. Her voice was filled with enthusiasm as she described what she was learning. Jeanie noted that the hobby was something she'd never considered before. This particular time was just right and her interest was inspired.

I commented on how much I was enjoying her wholehearted response to her new endeavor and she made an insightful remark that really struck me to the core. She said, "I love learning."

A simple comment, but it awoke a similar feeling I'd experienced at times, not realizing then that the feeling was the joy of learning. I love that!

There are so many layers of understanding in this scenario. I'll share a few that struck me; I'm sure as you read this, you'll see more.

First of all, the simple joy of learning. Joy comes from direct contact with our innate mental health. Joy is inherent. How wonderful that is—the naturalness and joy of learning. I've been feeling this more as my understanding deepens, but never put a name to it. I just feel good much of the time. I love when insights pop into my mind and I see something new that enhances life.

The second thing that occurred to me is that joy and learning keep us young and vital. Both Jeanie and I are seniors, yet we seldom notice this. We're having too much fun in life. Of course, there are mornings when I rise and there may be a few aches before my body loosens up and is ready for the day, but it's minor.

The third benefit I noticed is that, for the most part, even when I'm going through some stressful thinking, there is more an observer quality to my thinking; less attachment to my personal thoughts. Living in joy brings clarity and understanding. Again, I love this and am so grateful.

Learning comes in many disguises. I'll tell you a story that may bring a smile to your face. I'm not fond of technology; although I love what new technology offers, I have a blind spot when it comes to learning new systems. I've long held the thought that because I don't understand technology and I'm not good at reading instructions, technology is challenging for me to learn.

I like Ken to set things up for me and once that's done, I'm good to go. Ken is always encouraging me to follow through on my own, and sometimes I do, and the joy of learning feeds me and opens my mind so I "get" things more quickly. But there are still times when my thoughts of "I don't get this newfangled tech stuff" get in my way and make learning difficult. At that point, I feel and sound like a crotchety old lady!

I bought a new IPod just before Christmas and asked the clerk at the store to give me one that was especially simple to use. "User friendly," I said. I like to play Syd's early audio tapes and some of my favorite music when I'm traveling.

The clerk assured me the model he was demonstrating was the very thing. Some of what he said made sense so I thought, "I can handle this." Clutching my new purchase, I made my way home, excited to try it out. Ken very kindly set it up for me, loading my recordings and so on. I plugged in my headphones and pressed the various icons. No sound; I kept on but to no avail—still couldn't hear a thing. In frustration and saying a few choice words under my breath, I asked Ken for tech support.

He valiantly did his best but he couldn't hear any of my play lists either. Then I went online to get the user's manual. The device only came with a tiny folder of instructions that needed a magnifying glass in order to be read. I couldn't find the right model number online, etc. etc. etc. You get the picture. There was no joy in learning here!

Finally, I decided to go back to the store and ask for their help. That decision stabilized me, and my annoyance vanished. I felt good at taking charge and off I went. The clerk was a little harried as this was the day before Christmas and he was busy. I patiently waited for him until he plugged the device cord into his mini speakers on the counter, adjusted and pressed things on the screen and the sound came clear as a bell.

I asked to start the IPod from scratch myself, while in the store, to ensure that I could do this. Everything went well. I was tickled. I skipped out of the store, drove home, told Ken all was well, plugged in my headphones—couldn't hear a thing! Oh my.

I had to set the monster device aside until a couple of days later, then asked Ken if he would go back to the store with my IPod and ask for help. I felt so foolish that I couldn't get this to work, and felt Ken would stand a better chance of understanding this difficult technical challenge. With great forbearance, he agreed.

He came back smiling like a Cheshire cat. "What's the problem?" I asked. Ken chuckled as he informed me that I hadn't plugged the headphones in far enough, nor had he! When we tried earlier, the connection had felt stiff, and we didn't want to force it. Once they were inserted properly, I could hear the sound perfectly. Joy reigned in my heart and in our home.

More lessons learned: Be patient, let wisdom take the reins, back off from negative feelings. Then the joy of learning naturally fills our being. New learning and new beginnings for the New Year!

CHAPTER 36
SEEING INNATE PHYSICAL HEALTH MANIFEST

When I had my first insight into the nature of emotion, realizing that emotion comes from our ability to think, it was a watershed moment in my life. Previous to that, I thought my all-encompassing circumstances were the sole reason I felt as I did about my life. I had no concept that my thinking created my reality. Once I had the insight, my life was enhanced immeasurably.

As time went on, I could see more and more evidence of the Three Principles at work in my life and consequently, how they worked in the rest of humanity. I began to see how to nourish my mental well-being, how to focus on the positive rather than the negative. Being in charge of my thinking was such a novel activity; it was inspiring and empowering to be the master of my domain.

Over the years, I naturally slipped into counting on wisdom to help me spiritually and psychologically, intuitively trusting that wisdom comes from the spiritual realm and is always present, even when I may be out to lunch, figuratively speaking. I continue to nourish wisdom, to love and honor the spiritual core within, as best I can.

There were phases when I had a glimmer of innate physical health rising to the surface, times when I really listened to what my body needed, and I responded to the need to eat healthy foods in order to be physically healthy. Then my old habits of thinking of food, usually junk food, as providing comfort as opposed to nourishment would slip into my reality again and I would lose sight of my natural physical ability to be healthy.

I kept hearing about inflammation being the root cause of so many diseases or health concerns. I dismissed what I was hearing. But wisdom niggled me and prodded me to do some research. The information I found opened my mind; it made sense. It came to me that although I'm fine with aging and I celebrate it, I wasn't fine with infirmity. I didn't want to walk with a cane, if I could help it. If I couldn't, fine. I'd be grateful to have something to assist me. But I wasn't quite ready yet.

Then I had an insight that there is a natural physical well-being that is innate as well as our inherent spiritual, psychological health. I began to see I could count on my physical immune system, if I listened to it, in the same way I count on wisdom to support me, if I listen to it.

What made this real are the physical results I experienced when I listened to my body, to my natural immune system. When I listened and ate healthier, eliminating foods that weren't good for me, I could see it was the same as dismissing negative thoughts. My wisdom had space to reveal itself, both mentally and physically. I found alignment between the form and formless; Oneness became more apparent and practical as well as profound.

That insight made all the difference. This was evolutionary for me. All my life, I've struggled with weight issues, and related health concerns, the same as my parents. Given the way I was brought up, the heavy, fatty foods we consumed seemed normal. I didn't see them as unhealthy. However, as I aged, and arthritis increased as well as other health problems, I just related it to aging. When it became apparent I would need a cane to walk, I thought, "So be it." However, I wasn't happy about it.

I'm beyond grateful that my wisdom prevailed and wouldn't let up until my intellect "got" the logic of wisdom, both inside and out. I *see* there are common sense principles that underlie the physical condition as well as spiritual Principles that underlie the mental and physical state. The insight about my physical health came from the spiritual. These natural internal and external guidance systems are gifts for us to use wisely. My understanding deepened and I saw a parallel between the inner and the outer realm.

An example: While on vacation recently, I wondered how I would do at an "all inclusive" resort. I wasn't sure I could handle it, despite having listened to my body for several months, eating healthier, and experiencing reduced inflammation, barely noticeable arthritis, and no heartburn, all symptoms which had been a daily complaint. An added bonus I hadn't been looking for was weight loss.

The first week, I was strong in my physical well-being. It wasn't difficult. I just picked healthy food from the abundant buffet and was quite satisfied. The second week, old habits crept back in; I began to eat less healthily, immediately got heartburn, and didn't feel well. Much as I'd rather not admit this, the unhealthy foods tasted delicious! It was the after affects that were not good.

I talked with Ken about this and he said, "Don't worry about it. You're doing so much better than ever before. If you can't indulge occasionally and then go back to your healthy life style when you return home, there's something wrong."

He was absolutely right. When I returned home, I naturally fell back into my healthier food habits, continued to walk as exercise, and heartburn and other symptoms disappeared. It wasn't hard at all. There was an extra protection from the insight about our natural physical immune system working for us.

I continue to learn about these old habits of eating healthy or not healthy. What I can say is, there is a definite orientation toward health even though I veer off occasionally. Arthritis is minimal and has been for some time. When I slip into unhealthy eating, I do my best not to beat myself up.

I am seeing a parallel in how it becomes easier to slip from a bad mood psychologically into mental well-being, once we have more wisdom in the "bank" as a foundation. It's exactly the same with physical well-being. The more we listen to the wisdom of our bodies, the more physical health we have as a foundation. The resilience is there, allowing us to bounce back without effort. I'm in awe of this and once again, exceedingly grateful.

CHAPTER 37
TOO MUCH FUN?

It's fascinating to me how deeply hidden our beliefs can be. I remember Sydney Banks saying to me, "*Once you have an insight, you've only touched the tip of the iceberg. There is much more hidden beneath the water.*" He went on to say that an insight will eliminate beliefs we may have carried for a lifetime and in doing so, open the door to new understanding.

Once again his words have proven true. I never realized before that I had thought wisdom could be fun, but not too much fun. . . .I felt wisdom was found more in the realm of profundity.

Yes, I certainly became more lighthearted once I discovered who I was on the inside and began to *see* the Principles manifest in my life. But it was only a couple of years ago when I realized I had an intellectual belief that I shouldn't have too much fun. I thought too much fun was frivolous and unworthy of wisdom. Yes, lighthearted and joyful but too much fun? Well, one has to watch that. . .

Wow! What an eye opener that insight was, that when you are in integrity to Self, the seemingly impossible happens and the door to fun really opens wide.

I was afforded the opportunity to meet my daughter and daughter-in-law in Bali. I gladly accepted, and made arrangements to go in August.

Now here's the "too much fun" part. They told me they were heading to Barcelona and other parts of Spain after Bali. I got a feeling I'd love to accompany them, if they were into me joining them. When I asked how they felt about this, their response touched my heart. They were thrilled to have me continue my travels with them.

When I spoke to Ken, he said "Why not?" He wasn't going with me but totally encouraged me. I started to get a little scared. Approval from my husband and my family—oh my! I started to pull back, thinking this is too much of a good thing for me. However I casually decided to do some exploration about how to change my return ticket and a number of other details that needed attention. It began to look difficult. Surprise!

I said to Ken that I thought these new travel arrangements wouldn't work. He said, "Just sit with it." His words settled me and I followed his advice. The thought popped into my mind to try one more time to see about changing my ticket. This time around, it was simple. My inquiries produced results. I had said to myself before I began my research that if things flow, then it's right that I go. Things flowed. . .I went to Bali, Lombok, and Barcelona.

The journey was fabulous, an adventure of a lifetime, bonding me with my daughter/daughter-in-law in a way we'd never experienced before.

What came to me later is that I thought I wasn't worthy to have fun and such good fortune. How about those hidden beliefs! Talk about the rest of the iceberg submerged under water.

Thank you, Sydney Banks!

CHAPTER 38
DEAR ELSIE,

At the program today, you spoke in a way I've never heard before. I have read your books and watched videos of you before and always enjoyed them, but today something different happened. I heard you today. And I felt the impulse to write you.

I heard something; I am not sure what it is. It sounded like: wisdom is inside, trust wisdom. I really heard that; it was magical, I saw it in myself. I felt it. I'd heard it thousands of times before, but now it was different; it was true, not a nice sounding commonplace phrase, it was deep, it was there. Wisdom always works for me and for everybody else. I saw this wisdom inside for the split of a second. Wisdom is me, it is not some supernatural force to be invoked and that sometimes comes to help and sometimes doesn't. I also saw how unworthy of wisdom I feel most of the time and this is when I get away from it.

I am so moved right now. I don't really have words; it's like something beyond the reality of thought, something fundamental, beyond judgment or should do's. It's beyond getting caught up in petty little mind games. It was such depth in your words, such a deep understanding and connection, I am just in awe. I would have liked to hear you talk forever like that.

Thank you from all my heart! Ioana.

Chapter 39
Victoria's Email

Elsie, thank you for gracing us with your presence and joining in conversation with us. You added so much that so many resonated with, including me. When you said that we "are" wisdom, that led to an avalanche of insights, and in fact, I would say an epiphany for me. Something inside me clicked and there was an instant recognition of being that wisdom; how I am God energy, how we all are, and what that means in our human form.

The epiphany that I had blows my mind. I have, in my 58 years, always had a shield between me and other people. I would have moments of connection and periods of trust but there was always something there where I felt less than, unworthy, and needed to shield myself from criticism and judgment (*as if others' criticism and judgment mean anything*).

What I experienced, what I "saw" is amazing. You talked about disguises that people put on. What I realized is that I have been putting a costume on top of those disguises. Then I would react to the costume that I created. And in that moment of your comment I saw through the costume I put on everyone; and through their disguise, and now literally see everyone as they truly are; God source. I wish I could convey the impact and the truth of this for me. But suffice it to say it is life-changing.

These last few days I have not reacted but instead have responded to people. Imagine, there's nothing to react to anymore! Reacting to that costume that I put on others would be like trying to scare myself, looking in the mirror going "Boo!"

How fun this is to enjoy the costumes and disguises and not take them seriously (*as real*) because of what I see and feel behind that. And what I see and feel is peace and pure love.

With deep love and appreciation, Victoria.

CHAPTER 40
WE'RE ALWAYS AT *HOME*

My time recently has been rich with discovery, and continues to unfold. The previous two letters were written by Ioana and Victoria, who were part of a program at which I'd spoken. Both women shared so beautifully and profoundly that I felt their insights were important to share, and with their permission, offer them here.

I am moved to share my own insights about wisdom truly being inside us all. There is never a time when we aren't connected to wisdom or Mind.

For a while now I've been seeing more fully that we are truly *home* all the time, no matter the challenges we face, or troubling thoughts we may have. There is an underlying spiritual protection comforting and guiding us, our true nature offering solace and solutions.

For a long time, I found myself talking about wisdom "having my back" or being "shoulder to shoulder" with me. Those phrases were expressions of how wisdom felt to me. The conundrum is that I would also talk about wisdom being "inside" of us. It began to dawn on me that if wisdom is inside, why was I making wisdom sound as if it were outside of me by it having my back, and so on?

Knowing that wisdom/home is who we are and where we are has brought more simplicity and harmony to my life. There isn't the duality of being "inside" or "outside." There is the feeling of Oneness, a wholeness, seeing a single coin with two sides blending seamlessly and harmoniously. The formless and the form being One.

I find that even when I'm having troubling thoughts, I no longer feel like I'm outside of myself. There's no place to go. It feels more like I'm still at *home* and may be at the periphery of my understanding, yet still *home*. It's reassuring and lessens the feeling of stress, the illusionary pressure of having to do something to get back "home."

There is a relaxation, a slipping into the space of understanding.

As I shared with the group that Ioana and Victoria were part of, the feeling of wisdom infused the room. The deep feeling was so strong it felt as if it had substance, that you could reach out and touch something solid. At the same time, it felt light and very moving emotionally. Many people shared insights they'd had in the moment. Others shared their insights a few days later in emails, as did Ioana and Victoria.

There is no question that everyone in the room felt a degree of this combined expression of our true nature/wisdom manifesting. Although several participants spoke about the feeling as if it was coming from me, I continued to point back to their wisdom rising to the surface and resonating with all.

I've heard this deep feeling referred to as a "contact high." Some may think this feeling won't last or that it's not possible to have it again, without being with charismatic speakers or in the presence of many others on the same journey.

That's not so. I can't emphasize this enough. That deep feeling is our true nature expressing itself. If we dismiss it as a "contact high," that's what it will be. If we celebrate and honor our inner core, that part of us that is spiritual essence and connected to Mind, *is* Mind, It will continue to offer wisdom and solutions to guide us in life. Even when we're not listening. . . .despite our personal thinking, wisdom remains central and foundational to our very being.

CHAPTER 41
HIDDEN INSIGHTS

I love talking with people who are new to the Three Principles. They have freshness and curiosity that sometimes imperceptibly fades as we gain more understanding about what life is, and what and who we are on the "inside."

There are times when I begin to take my understanding for granted. I'm so grateful Mind looks after us at those times by offering an opportunity to see something fresh; something that brings forth a renewed perspective.

Such an opportunity presented itself recently. I had the pleasure of speaking with someone who was relatively new to the Principles understanding. I'll call my new friend "Roy." At one point, I asked him what had touched him about the Principles. Roy spoke briefly about current self-improvement modalities that he had explored and went on to say he wasn't really sure what had drawn him to the Principles. When he first heard about this work, he thought it was similar to what he'd already been trained in. Yet something kept him coming back and exploring with more depth.

Roy continued to ponder my question about what drew him, and finally said he couldn't put his finger on any one thing he'd heard. He went on to describe how his coaching with clients had changed; how he could no longer offer his old traditional coaching techniques. He spoke of being rather awkward in his conversations with clients because he didn't know how to talk about the Principles. He mentioned the emotional response one of his clients experienced, which released an enormous amount of stress and brought out her wellbeing, and a degree of understanding of the correlation between her thinking and her experience.

In a matter of fact tone, Roy told me similar responses had occurred in many of his clients. To me, this clearly illustrated that

Roy's clients had heard something of value during their coaching conversations.

Roy didn't seem to make the same connection. He saw the results, but seemed to feel that because he wasn't completely comfortable talking about the Principles, the results were secondary rather than primary.

My new friend also mentioned the profound feelings he often experiences now, that he hadn't had before. He concluded, "I can't tell you what I've seen or heard about the Principles. I don't know that I've had any insights."

This story absolutely delighted me! Clearly, the fact that Roy noticed the relief his humble coaching had brought to others was insightful. Equally obvious were the deep and rich feelings he was experiencing. Roy was living more of the time in contentment, even though he told me he and his family had faced some life challenges.

As I shared my observations with my colleague, we both began to laugh. Cosmic humor had played a joke on this dear man. Roy was doing wonderful work from the seemingly hidden world of insight and didn't even know it.

That's how subtle and natural insight can be. *Seeing* indicates insight in the moment. We *see* from wisdom, our default setting, and often times, don't even realize it. It's like that old saying "You can't see the forest for the trees."

The same thing happened to me recently while I was traveling extensively, sharing the Principles with various groups. I've never felt so in the moment; never enjoyed my life more. I went from place to place, meeting new and familiar friends. I wasn't hanging on mentally to the previous event. Every moment was full and complete. It was wholly captivating. This wasn't a conscious effort; it just happened. I became aware of this mental space after the fact.

While traveling, I didn't have insights I could put my finger on. I just had a smile on my face and in my heart the whole time, as I journeyed on the train from London, admiring the beautiful Devon countryside. The same in-the-moment experience continued throughout my adventure, doing programs in Exeter and in

Edinburgh. I loved my time with new and dear friends in both places.

The highlight was having the privilege of speaking on a panel at the Scottish Parliament, featuring Sydney Banks' work. There was such a dream-like quality to that experience. While we were speaking, Syd's face from a video was shown on several screens around the room and one above our heads. The screens were softly lit so his face appeared as if emerging from the mists of time. It was magical.

As momentous as that event was, time moved on, and when the meeting concluded, I continued to move forward in the flow of life. Occasionally, the event came to mind again, and I would shake my head in wonder. What would Syd have thought of this historic gathering at Parliament, convened to share the results of a new mental health paradigm he'd uncovered in a spontaneous epiphany? I could only continue to be in wonder.

Lastly, I was privileged to have the opportunity to explore the magical city of Edinburgh, Sydney Banks' birthplace; to wander the streets, my mind quiet and resting, simply absorbing the sights as beauty filled my senses.

My mind wasn't filled with "stuff;" it wasn't filled with insights. It's as if the insights were hidden until they appeared in the moment when I was in service, responding to the need, speaking with people. . . . So wisdom was/is still serving—just in a different way than I'd experienced before. I didn't know that having nothing on my mind— nothingness—could feel so rich and fulfilling.

Life is full, contentment reigns; still a bit challenging at times, just enough to keep one humble, realizing that there's always more to learn. Mind continues to teach us that we're always "home." And even though I can't really put my finger on any insights I had while away. . . I'm good with the simplicity of wisdom unfolding in its own way.

CHAPTER 42
SHARING IN SHORTHAND

A young friend asked me a question a couple of months after my talk at the Tikun Innate Health Conference in London that took place in May 2016. She said, "You talked about 'sharing in shorthand.' Could you say more about that?"

I'd forgotten about the content of that talk until she mentioned it. As she recalled some of the points I'd spoken about, it started to come back to me.

My plenary session, shared with a colleague, was on the last day of the conference. I'd been so moved by the depth of many of the presenters as they spoke profoundly about the spiritual nature of life.

That morning, driving to the conference venue with other presenters, I got very quiet and didn't engage in the general conversation. I was reflecting on what my talk would be about. I had a title, but no content. . . My mind was empty. I felt like an empty vessel, and to be perfectly candid, it felt rather unnerving.

It seemed to me everything had been covered by other presenters. I had nothing to add. I'd observed over the last couple of years that more presenters were comfortable sharing their understanding about the spiritual nature of the Principles. To speak to the spiritual nature of life has always been my favorite topic, so I wasn't sure what I could offer that hadn't already been said.

I was in a quiet quandary. As I walked down the hallway toward the main conference room, I came upon another colleague I'd not had an opportunity to speak with yet. We stopped to chat.

"How are you doing?" I asked.

"Fine," he said. "How about you?"

"Fine," was my response. Then my colleague said, "I'm not really." And began to share what he was feeling in the moment; that he also was wondering what would come out of him for his topic.

His honesty struck a responding chord in me and we began to share at a deep level. It was a very brief exchange but we were both very moved by the feeling of connection.

We carried on to the main room and soon it was time for my talk. The only thing I could share was my honesty about not knowing what to say, that I felt an empty vessel, and that I felt everyone else had done such an amazing job of sharing the essence of the Principles understanding that there was nothing left to say.

And then it came to me about sharing in "shorthand" and how this quality of sharing has the power to take people home, to their spiritual birthplace. The feeling that comes from within is true nature speaking to true nature.

Common long hand phrases came to mind: "living in the feeling of our thinking;" "reconnecting to Mind;" "I see that my stress is caused by my thinking but that's not doing me any good."

It struck me in the moment that we can shorten "living in the feeling of our thinking" to "living in the feeling," and then shorten it even more to "living." This paring down to the essence of experience removes all the distraction of words. It's not that the information contained in the sentence isn't valuable. Indeed, it is very valuable. It's just that at a certain point, too much explanation can be a slippery slope—the slippery slope into personal analysis. Once you know that thought creates experience, forget it! Just live.

This *knowing* offers freedom from our personal thinking, from trying to figure out why we are where we are, and how we are doing psychologically. Sharing in shorthand leads to learning in shorthand; there is less word distraction, thus clearing the way for insight. In other words, shorthand learning eliminates psychological analysis and provides space for peace of mind and insightful understanding.

Remember how Syd always talked about true knowledge being beyond the word? Well, I feel this shorthand learning/sharing is a glimmer of that knowledge.

"Reconnecting to Mind" is a common phrase that is rather misleading. We're always connected to Mind; there's never a time we're not connected. We are part of Mind and Mind is our essence.

So to say "reconnecting" infers that we're disconnected; an innocent, well-meaning phrase that can be of concern to people. *Knowing* we're always connected brings reassurance that we're always living at home. *Knowing* this brings solace and insight.

"I see that my stress is caused by my thinking but that's not doing me any good." I've heard this sentence numerous times. I've said this phrase myself numerous times! What I've come to realize is that "I *see*" is the key point. The rest of the phrase is really immaterial.

Seeing is the Principle of Consciousness in action. When we focus on the fact that we *see*, we're home. We're home in our wisdom, our spiritual home: a space of understanding, contentment, and the ability to live in grace, no matter what comes our way.

CHAPTER 43
A Deeper Aspect of Consciousness

As a child, I was brought up in a religion that looked at consciousness very differently from the way Sydney Banks taught about the Principle of Consciousness. In my early religious education, I was taught to be conscious of my wrong-doings so I could repent, change my behavior, and be more in alignment with God. I was taught that we were all born in original sin. This scared me and kept me constantly on the look-out for my sins because if I died, depending on the severity of my sins, I would either end up in purgatory or hell. I seldom rested with an easy mind. Not a good state for a child to be in.

This way of looking only at my wrong-doings colored my whole life and the way I perceived my worthiness. I never felt good enough because I was always conscious of what was wrong in me and in my life rather than looking for what was good. Consequently, I had a great deal of judgment, not only of myself but of everyone I came in contact with.

As I matured and married, I continued to carry the same mind set. This way of looking at life didn't endear me to my husband, children, or friends. Most importantly, it didn't endear me to myself!

Fast forward to when I had my first insight that Thought creates feeling and I finally understood that I was the thinker. I began to see it wasn't my external circumstances that created my reality; it was the way I viewed and thought about my situation that formed my experience. I finally got a glimmer that I had some wisdom I'd previously been unaware of.

As my inner journey continued, I learned more about the Principle of Thought and how it worked, but still harbored questions about innate mental health and Consciousness.

When Syd talked to me about innate mental health and how

everyone is born with this spiritual gift, I found it hard to accept because of my strongly held religious beliefs. I told him about all the things that were wrong with me.

He was so kind in his response. Looking at me with gentleness in his eyes he said, *"Don't trouble yourself worrying about what you've done wrong, Elsie. When you become conscious of your True Self, you will find a whole new world, filled with beauty, understanding and love."*

I didn't have a clue what he meant when he spoke about True Self but I got a nice feeling when he said such things. So I pondered about this statement and then I pondered some more. The more I pondered, the less I understood.

The next time I got together with Syd for a cup of tea, I had a number of questions I wanted to ask him. I told him that his statement about innate mental health didn't fit with my belief in original sin, and I asked him how that could be.

His eyes weren't so gentle this time. With a bit of a frown, he said, *"Stop trying to figure it out, Elsie. Just listen for a feeling and the understanding will come. You can't find truth with your intellect. You find truth through a deep feeling which brings insight."*

Well that didn't help me at all in the moment, but as the day continued, I began to feel a sense of peace, almost despite myself. And a thought came to mind. Could this feeling of peace be what Syd was talking about? Was this feeling my True Self?

Although I didn't realize it then, that peace I experienced was more evidence that there was something inside me that was more powerful than me trying to figure things out.

After more reflection, I began to see that my awareness or consciousness of the peace I was feeling was tied to the Principle of Consciousness. Bingo! I began to see that Consciousness is more than the ability to 'bring our thinking to life,' although that is part of the role of Consciousness.

For me, the most powerful, deepest learning is that Consciousness is our awareness that we are form and formless. We are spiritual beings living in the physical form. This is our life's education; learning how to honor our spiritual nature while living in our human form, and honoring our human nature as an expression of our spiritual essence via Thought. This is the gold for me.

Sydney Banks says in *The Missing Link*, "*Consciousness allows the recognition of form, form being the expression of Thought.*"

He goes on to say, "*Pure soul and pure consciousness can only temporarily be separated by the erroneous thoughts of humanity because soul and consciousness are one and the same.*"

CHAPTER 44
IN THE BOXING RING WITH PERSONAL THINKING

There's nothing like a bout with one's personal thinking to bring about a fresh appreciation for the power of thought; especially when life has been feeling blissful. A situation occurs and before we know it, we are gripped by our imagination gone awry, and start flailing at our opponent in the ring of our thoughts. When we're gripped this tightly, we may not realize our opponent is none other than ourselves!

It's not an experience I relish; it's an experience that tempers and humbles and makes one stronger, in the sense of seeing there is always more to learn, and that sometimes the learning isn't gentle.

Feeling judgment of another is rooted in expectation and ego, and when that individual doesn't respond in the way we expect, disappointment and upset charge into the ring with determination that whomever we're upset with is in the wrong and we are right!

Oh my, what a battle. No one is the winner. It's not until we are weary of the negative feelings that some balance comes back into our reality and we regain our footing. Our spinning world slows and peace enters, soothing the intellect so understanding seeps through.

Once again, wisdom reigns. The path is clear. Nothing is accomplished through judgment and blame. What is helpful is knowing that we don't want to learn in that harsh manner. It's unnecessary, yet it served its purpose. Realizing we don't want that unhealthy feeling lifts the rope barrier around the self-imposed ring.

Freedom! We experience feelings of relief, gratitude, and appreciation that we don't live in the web of judgment all the time, like we used to. A brief interlude with negativity showcases the harmony of living in wisdom.

CHAPTER 45
I — SEE —THOUGHT

In my mentoring of new students or clients, they will often start off our conversations sharing how they see their thinking is creating their stress, adding much pressure to their lives, and contributing to unhappy relationships.

It came to me during one of these conversations that if people *realize* the fact that they *see* it's their thinking creating their stress, this insight would instantly relieve their anxiety. It's about moving past the form of thought to *seeing* the creative power of thought as a Principle.

It's about moving past personal consciousness of what they're seeing to the neutrality of *seeing* the Principle of Consciousness, which is the awareness of our experience and most importantly, of who is creating our experience—us!

This understanding would shorten the following sentence. Instead of "I see my thinking is creating my stress/pressure/messed up relationships," consider this: I—SEE—THOUGHT:

I = Mind,

SEE = Consciousness,

THOUGHT = Create.

The Three Principles acting in unison to create experience. The rest of the sentence, "my stress/pressure/messed up relationships" is the form of thought.

Stick to the Principles; they are before form, where creation happens in the moment. *Seeing* this brings freedom from all our thinking. *Seeing* this releases us from judgment of what we're thinking. It keeps us grounded in the Principles, where wisdom resides, providing ease in life.

Seeing is the key word in this topic. *Seeing* happens when we are living inside, in the core of our being, our true nature. The phrase,

"Our thinking is doing this or that" is living outside, in the form of thought. It's being stuck in the experience rather than living in the moment of creation.

When we *see* this we are moved by the simplicity and by wonder. We are the creator of our experience, which means we always have the freedom of choice. We have the power of Mind; we are Mind. When we're part of something, we can't be divorced or separated from it, even when we're momentarily living "outside."

"What if your thoughts are continually creating an experience of lack of money?" is a question someone asked. The questioner went on to say, "Other things are improving; relationships, attitudes about life, how I view my career, etc... but the money part remains stubbornly stuck in 1st gear and seemingly won't budge. Do I need to figure out what I'm thinking and stop that thought? It doesn't feel like thought when I look at my bank account and rent, and the bills that are due right now. It feels very real."

What struck me about this question/comment is that the questioner's life is improving. I love that! When we see and are grateful for "what is," then the "what isn't" begins to improve as well! When our attention shifts to being grateful for what has changed in our life, challenging issues begin to look different as our perspective changes. It takes faith that this is so. Faith leads to results.

I've had that experience in my own life. A few years back, I was fixated on getting more work, more clients, more understanding, more, more, more. It seemed what I had just wasn't enough, and in the reality of paying bills, it's true we were struggling to meet the mortgage and so on.

This continued for some time, until one day the light went on and the phrase came to me, "When is enough, enough?" It occurred to me that all I was focused on was what was wrong in my life, especially the lack of financial comfort.

There were other great things happening, but I didn't see them, as my thoughts were focused on lack, not abundance. Somehow, my human nature became so enamored with "more" that I'd temporarily forgotten that less is more... When that insight landed, my life changed.

I won't say life changed overnight. First of all, it was the feeling that changed, the feeling of gratitude for what I did have, not bothered so much by what I didn't have. We'd eaten rice and beans before, and were happy to do so, as we were living in the dream of being in service to the world, sharing the gift of these Principles.

The insight broadened for me, illuminating that while I was concentrating on achieving more, whether work, money, or better life, I wasn't truly being in service to myself, or to the world.

The primary purpose of the gift of the Principles, as I see it, is to share the gift freely, without thought of what you'll get back. Please don't misunderstand. I don't mean not to charge a fee for your work. I mean, don't let making money be your main concern.

When you give freely, Mind will provide, more than you can imagine. Give the gift, and you will receive. And I did. When the feeling I was living in changed, as if by magic, the feeling of love, of being in service, brought abundance. Once again, the feeling of essence did the work.

I'll wrap this up by saying one more time:

I—SEE—THOUGHT.

Simple, direct, profound—the answer to all life's questions.

CHAPTER 46
BE OPEN TO OPPORTUNITY

When we evolve in our spiritual understanding, we gain more knowledge about the psychological workings of our everyday life. For example, one may feel the desire to share what they've learned about the Three Principles but be uncertain how to begin. The biggest thing is to be open to opportunity when it presents itself.

I remember being offered an opportunity to develop a program for Juvenile Justice and initially turning them down. I suggested they approach another individual who was trained in that field. I didn't have any background in Juvenile Justice and felt out of my depth in putting together a program for a group I'd never worked with. My insecurity was on high alert!

Something niggled at me during the phone conversation I had with the Deputy Chief of the division so I continued to listen, even though everything inside me was saying "No, I don't do this kind of work." Perhaps it was when she said that the person I'd recommended to her, who was familiar with juvenile corrections, had in fact referred her to me. I began to listen, rather than blocking what she was offering.

As I listened, I heard the enthusiasm in her voice about what the new Principles paradigm offered. She and a group from the county had visited another state where there was an ongoing, very successful Principles based program in place. She was struck by the results that were occurring, with reduced recidivism from the youth, and more open conversation about innate mental health that was the primary focus between the probation officers, counselors, and incarcerated adolescents.

I became captivated by her enthusiasm and my insecurity lessened. I found myself offering to speak with a cross section of department heads from the Juvenile Justice division to get a feeling for what they were looking for.

That call with the group eliminated the rest of my insecurity and long story short, I gratefully agreed to develop a three day training as an introduction to the Principles, to see if there was enough interest in the staff to move forward and progress to a yearlong training of trainers program.

It was an amazing project that I'll never forget. I learned so much from the whole group and especially from the youngsters who were in detention. To see them cautiously open up to being viewed as innately mentally healthy by officers and counselors was very stirring to me and to the Deputy Chief and County Commissioners. Many of these children had been in and out of detention many times and had a very fixed viewpoint that they were considered "bad" and needed to be "fixed."

To be taught they had innate mental health as their default setting, something they could always count on, especially on the "outside" when temptation was strongest, was a solid foundation they took with them when they were released.

Not only did their new found understanding show them that they were innately wise and mentally healthy, their growing confidence and peace of mind was an undeniable result that moved their parents, siblings, and friends, for the most part, to a new vantage point of feeling hopeful; for many of them, for the first time in their lives. Thus the reduction and sustainability in recidivism afforded all a new opportunity for the future.

This also demonstrated to me that the outer disguise of any social or business endeavor isn't the key element in whether one can share their understanding of the Principles. The key element is that underneath the disguise, we're all the same spiritual essence. This is what we speak to, not to the outer workings. When our consciousness is stirred and awoken, the outer workings naturally change to healthy, productive living.

Such is the gift of these precious Principles that Sydney Banks uncovered.

CHAPTER 47
THE POWER OF INSIGHT

During a fascinating and insightful conversation with a client, the power of insight took on a fresh and deeper meaning for me.

My client, let's call her Penelope, related some profound insights she'd had as a writer; how her writing was inspired and driven by insight, and how the writing seemed effortless when inspired. I understand exactly what she means, as I experience the same in my writing. Like Penelope, when I'm moved by insight, my writing seems to write itself. I love the freedom and the feeling of this experience, and I'm very grateful for this gift.

Penelope went on to say that although she experienced the flow of inspiration in writing, her mind was cluttered with thoughts of failure in other areas of her life; her financial situation was precarious, her relationship with her partner was stressed, and a variety of other personal dilemmas were taking place.

"Why is my world in such turmoil? I thought once I learned about the Principles, I'd have less stress and my life would straighten out. Yet here I go again down that same path of not knowing where my next paycheck is coming from. My partner tells me not to worry, but how can I not worry when we can't make the mortgage payment this month. I don't understand why this keeps happening to me," Penelope lamented.

As I listened to her, my heart was touched by her feeling of futility and it occurred to me that she wasn't seeing the connection between having an insight in one part of her life, and how that insight will then overlap all aspects of life, if you allow it. The exact same power of Mind that provides insight in one area is available to guide you in all areas.

Penelope told me she realized she was being inspired from Mind in her writing, yet she couldn't make the transition into other areas of her life. She was more focused on what was missing than what she already had—the inspiration she was experiencing in her writing.

What prevents this insightful power from manifesting? The short and sweet answer is that our personal thinking gets in the way, coupled with a lack of gratitude. Interestingly, our personal thinking is coming from the same infinite power; it's just that we are using it against ourselves instead of for our benefit.

During our conversation, Penelope continued to voice her concern about the parts of her life that weren't working. She continued to say, "I know, I know," when I would point to the insights she'd shared with me.

My mind was still for a moment or two. "If you hold these spiritual gifts close to your heart and are grateful for what you've learned, rather than focusing on what you desire to learn, this position of having an open mind will go a long way to help you move forward in your learning."

Once again Penelope said, "I know." This was one too many times. "You don't know!" I said firmly. "If you knew, your life wouldn't be as you describe it. You wouldn't be stressed out as you are now. Stop and listen for a moment." There was a lengthy pause. I let the pause continue as I knew that finally she was listening.

"Okay, I'm with you." A different tone of voice accompanied Penelope's words, and I knew she had touched home base and was ready to learn. In that moment, it occurred to me to stop our session right there; to let her bathe in her own wisdom. I recommended this to her, adding that we would continue our conversation in a week or so. She readily agreed, and again I heard quietness in her voice that hadn't been there before.

Another thing Penelope was concerned about was that her insights lasted only a moment or two; therefore she thought it was a momentary understanding. Penelope didn't realize that insight brings about lasting change, even though she was experiencing that change in her writing. Because she wasn't feeling that shift in other parts of her life, she felt the insights were temporary. Penelope wasn't connecting the dots, which often happens. We don't always see the change in ourselves until someone else points it out.

An insightful moment is to be cherished, no matter that it is just a moment or two. It's like an eternity, in spiritual time. Let's not forget the fact that Sydney Banks' epiphany lasted only a few moments, and not only changed his world, but provided a new paradigm of understanding for the field of mental health, and for the world at large, for generations to come.

Shifting our orientation toward what is working rather than what isn't working is the best way to connect the dots in our life. It's that simple! Remember, we are creating our reality via our thoughts. So when we are consistently focusing on what is wrong, that is what shows up for us. When we shift our orientation (thoughts) to what is right, that is what shows up for us.

I know this to be true, as that is what happened to me. Years ago, if you had looked in the dictionary for a definition of "despair" you would have seen my photo, with a forlorn looking face, sad eyes, no energy. I was filled with despair and distress, feeling life was over for me, before it had really begun. I was innocently using this profound, transcendent power of Mind, Consciousness, and Thought against myself.

"Is this all there is?" was my constant refrain. Is it any wonder, given that we have the power to create our own experience, that my reality showed up as "Yes, that's all there is!"

My turning point was the insight: *Thought creates feeling.* That insight came in a split second of clarity during the lowest point of my life. I've never returned to despair since that moment. Certainly I've had low times when I felt sorry for myself, felt that'd I'd lost my way. But underlying those thoughts was this little light of *knowing* that I'm more than my thinking. I'm the creator of my reality.

Moving from the form of thinking to the power of creation is beyond description. Suffice to say that it starts with a shift in orientation; in other words, with insight, which provides understanding of who and what we really are. Knowing that Mind, Consciousness, and Thought are active in each and every insight, without exception, is one of the most powerful truths we can learn. We *are* the Principles in action. When we honor that spiritual fact, our lives transform and we live in grace.

CHAPTER 48
SPIRITUAL MARKETING

First of all, let me say that when I use the word "spiritual" and connect it to "marketing" I mean no disrespect to the spiritual nature of life, of humanity, or the spiritual nature of the Three Principles. My intent is not to make "spiritual" a product.

I write this to share the power, profundity and practicality of the richness of our true nature expressing itself via a deep feeling, and in doing so, awakening others to their own inner power or essence. It is in this awakening that practical solutions occur, driven by insight.

So often, I get calls from new practitioners who are concerned about how to start a business with the Three Principles as the foundation. They question their ability to articulate the Principles, thinking it's their words that will help their clients and bring in business. They share their anxiety while at the same time telling me they see it's their thinking that is getting in the way of moving forward with ease and confidence.

I love hearing them say "I see." As soon as I hear that phrase, I know they're *home* and they don't realize it. There is innocence in their lack of consciousness. However, their being *home* makes my job as a mentor easy. I just feel their essence and point to their oneness with that feeling.

It's cosmic irony that they are using the Principle of Consciousness but don't know it. Consciousness is the gift that never stops giving. Even when we don't see it, it's there stirring us, evoking new thought. And of course, Mind is at work in this situation, as is Thought. Mind is providing the light to *see*, and Thought is expressing the information.

The rich feeling of recognition that we are the Principles in action is the feeling and clarity that leads to healthy relationships and deep connection with others. It is the feeling of connection that attracts people and business. It's the feeling that conveys more than the words.

It's the feeling that opens the door to opportunities from "out of the blue." The deep feeling is where the magic happens. This is where "*doing without doing*" manifests with grace, simplicity, and ease.

It's so reassuring to know that we have what we need in the palm of our hand and in the core of our inner being. "*Once you have a glimmer of the Principles, just live and enjoy your life,*" Syd Banks often said, "*and you'll be taken care of.*"

I used to think that was too good to be true. Now I see that this is our default setting. Why wouldn't we honor the simplicity and truth of his message by doing exactly that? Just live!

CHAPTER 49
RESPECT WISDOM

Humanity is blessed to be imbued with a spiritual essence, filling us with feelings of love and understanding, as well as offering practical guidance for our everyday life. There is nothing more powerful or succinct than wisdom. In other words, our true nature is the epitome of clarity and compassion.

We slip into this rich feeling from time to time in a natural way; unsought and unexpected yet unmistakable as a profound feeling beyond our intellect.

Deep feeling is the connection; the bridge between the form and the formless nature of life. It's a fascinating journey to observe this connection, until we get caught up in the form—the outcome of wisdom—rather than living in an awareness of what wisdom is—spiritual essence.

When we respect what wisdom *is* rather than what wisdom does, our lives are transformed. We become so tuned in to our wisdom that everyday challenges are met with grace and ease (mostly). And when we do get caught up in our unhealthy thinking, there's more a feeling of being the observer rather than the victim. Being the observer neutralizes and defuses the tension.

This feeling of tension can be helpful, when it alerts us to the fact that we're moving too far from center, and reminds us to turn around and *see* who we are. This is how we learn; the interplay between our human nature and our spiritual nature. It's spiritual education, from the inside-out.

CHAPTER 50
THREE STEPS TO DEEPEN OUR UNDERSTANDING: PART ONE

One of the most frequent requests I get from practitioners and from ordinary people is to learn how to deepen their understanding (or said in another way, how to deepen their "grounding"). I ask them to tell me more about themselves so I can get a feel for how they see life. I'm interested in what they find most meaningful about the Principles, and how this understanding has helped them in their lives.

During the course of these conversations, I'm always struck by their wisdom as they remark on what they see and how they handle certain situations. Their wisdom shines forth and is clear to me. However, often times I see it is not clear to them. Their wisdom reveals itself in such a subtle, natural way that they don't see it, and so they miss one of the steps in deepening their understanding.

Step One: Acknowledge your wisdom.

To do this is simple. Quiet your mind by not entertaining all the noise available through the internet, social media, and so on. Leave space for your wisdom to emerge. When we slow down, wisdom will become more obvious to us.

For example: one client, we'll call her Carol, related how she'd been offered an amazing opportunity to do some Principles training for a large organization, specializing in serving those in crisis. At first she was delighted, and accepted the offer.

Then Carol's personal thinking kicked in and she became uncertain about her ability to handle this commission. Carol began to look for ways to edge out of the job, but held off. She carried on with her regular work for a couple of days, didn't check her emails or respond to the organization. Carol told me she felt calm, enjoyed her work and conversations.

Yet when Carol shared her story with me, her focus was on her personal thinking and the judgment she felt about her reluctance to take advantage of this great opportunity. Carol kept telling me, "What do I know about the Principles? I don't feel I have anything to share."

I asked Carol if she could see her wisdom in the story she told me. Carol kept repeating she couldn't believe how strung out she was by her personal thinking.

Does Carol sound strung out to you?

What I saw was that Carol's wisdom kept her calm, despite her personal thinking agitating her from time to time. Her wisdom kept her from turning down the opportunity. Her wisdom kept her from turning on her computer, allowing her to give her mind a break, allowing some space for wisdom to appear.

Carol didn't see this at all until I showcased it for her. Then her mind became still. The silence lasted for a few moments; then she got it. "Wow, I was totally focused on my thinking and didn't see my wisdom was at work, despite what I thought. I was calm, I was enjoying my life, I made several presentations and they were good. And yet I thought I was really stressed out."

Her insights brought a newly found confidence in trusting her wisdom, in acknowledging more fully its presence in her life. She realized more deeply that wisdom underlies our personal thinking and is always available. I know that Carol will be more sensitive, more conscious of her wisdom from now on.

She gleefully told me she was going to take the opportunity offered her.

It's fascinating to me that wisdom is right under our noses, so to speak, yet we often can't *see* it. Carol didn't see her wisdom because she was so focused on her personal thinking. Yet there is was, doing its job of keeping her on track.

Our experience changes, simply by focusing on our wisdom rather than our personal thinking. Sometimes it's hard because our personal thinking is so compelling. Nonetheless, if we consider this for just a moment, there are always flashes of light available to guide us. Honor those moments and they will grow.

This means it's not about us doing anything by will power—facing our fear and so on; it's about *seeing* (Consciousness). Then the doing is spontaneous, driven by insight.

CHAPTER 51
THREE STEPS TO DEEPEN OUR UNDERSTANDING: PART TWO

Sometimes insights are so subtle that people don't see the power contained in them. An example of this would be *realizing* one has a choice whether to engage in negativity, or to *see* it with understanding, which defuses the negative emotion.

Even with the new knowledge that they have a choice, people still may not get how valuable that is, and the transformative change it will produce in their behavior. It's like their intellect hasn't caught up with the difference in their internal workings, and they don't realize the full impact of what they have experienced.

I love pointing this out to my clients. I can see their thinking slow down as they get more reflective; then the penny drops and they begin to *see*. The insight becomes clear and obvious.

Step Two: Share your insights.

Sharing your insights takes you back inside to your wisdom, where deep feeling and more insights are waiting to be released. Sharing your insights brings the feeling of connection accompanied by deeper learning, for you and for those with whom you are sharing.

It's important and very helpful to know that people will *feel* you more than your words. When you share from the feeling of insight, the feeling released has the power to awaken others.

This is the gift of *feeling* in service—the deep feeling takes you beyond self-consciousness or uncertainty to knowing, even when you may not know what to say. It's a beautiful dichotomy that we can know the truth of an insight and yet be in the unknown in terms of how to share.

In this regard, a deep feeling of well-being is the foundation for connecting with others. It is primary—that deep feeling is an expression of our true nature, which has the power to awaken those with whom we come in contact. Deep feeling is the educator. The more we trust this when we're sharing, the more readily words will effortlessly come to mind, and we will often be surprised at what we say.

When we share, it's not necessarily about sharing or defining the Three Principles. That will come out when it's meant to. When Sydney Banks first shared his Enlightenment experience with Ken and me, one of the first things he shared was that he now knew what God was—Mind. He talked about how insecurity is simply Thought being used innocently against ourselves, and he pointed to and identified Consciousness as awareness of who and what we are.

Syd didn't talk about Three Principles until after the first psychologists came along to study with him. They pointed out that what he had uncovered were foundational Principles. This was a new term for Syd. Prior to that, he called Mind, Consciousness, and Thought "spiritual facts."

Because the Principles are formless energy, it really is difficult to explain them. It's more about the *feeling* that there is something deeper within. That deep feeling is what brings the Principles to life, and helps us comprehend and be able to articulate our understanding with more clarity and depth.

CHAPTER 52
THREE STEPS TO DEEPEN OUR UNDERSTANDING: PART THREE

Society tends to look at achievement as a measure of success. In our exploration of the Three Principles, we often continue that same tendency; to look for more—more understanding, more well-being, more peace, more, more, more. It's our human nature. This is the game of life.

Our human nature is always looking for more, while our spiritual nature is advising us to be grateful for what we have. How do we resolve this dilemma?

Once again, the answer is simple.

**Step Three: Be grateful for what you have learned,
rather than wishing for more.**

This speaks to being in the moment, present in our reality, whatever it is. If we're having a wonderful experience, there is an underlying feeling of appreciation just waiting to be recognized. If our experience is not so wonderful, we can still feel grateful we're *seeing* it and that we have a degree of understanding that our experience is coming from our own thinking. This understanding lessens the grip experience has on us; understanding gives us perspective. That's something to be grateful for.

Before I had any idea of who and what I am on the inside—a spiritual human being with the power to think and create—I was totally a victim of my own attitude toward life. I had no inkling that my experience had anything to do with me. When I had a spontaneous insight that my thoughts created my experiences, it was a transformative moment that completely changed the course of my life. When our lives are enriched as a result of insight, that's something to be grateful for.

As time went on after my first "Ah-ha" moment in the early days of my learning, my understanding seemed to vanish into thin air; I felt lost and at sea. In a way, it was worse than before, because I had experienced such peace of mind and then it seemed to disappear. What was up with that? I was definitely not feeling grateful for that presumed loss. . .

Syd happened to come over for a visit and saw my glum face. Much to my consternation, he didn't pay any attention to my moody demeanor. Instead, he began to tell me the latest news about how the Principles were spreading throughout the United States. He spoke in glowing terms about some of the psychologists who were having great results with their clients, and how more research to explore the efficacy of the Principles paradigm was happening on a national level.

It's rather embarrassing to say I got even gloomier. This news, although offering tremendous hope to the world, wasn't about me and how lost I was feeling. Syd's eyes twinkled as he continued his story and then offered to take me for lunch.

Over lunch, I simply forgot about my troubles, and my lost peacefulness re-emerged. I realized how blessed I was to be in the presence of, and having a conversation with, this Enlightened man.

I also realized that although I was stirred by Syd's wisdom, it was my own insights that brought a fresh perspective to my life. My soul danced with joy! Once again, I felt tethered to *home*. I realized more deeply that I am *home* all the time and that when I feel lost, I'm still nestled in my true nature—safe and sound.

I'm grateful to know that even when I'm out to lunch, figuratively speaking, at least I know that and it does give me comfort. I'm not mentally wandering around, aimlessly looking for what I already have within me, just as all humanity has within them. That's something to be forever grateful for, no matter what. What are you grateful for?

In summary, the three steps to deepen our understanding are: acknowledge our wisdom, share our insights, and be grateful for what we've found. These simple steps will ensure that we'll never stop our infinite journey of learning who and what we are at our spiritual core.

EPILOGUE

C oming to the end of the book has left me thoughtful, reflecting upon the legacy the late Sydney Banks left behind. As stated in the Dedication, I'm beyond fortunate to have traveled this extraordinary journey with an Enlightened being; one who was at the same time, ordinary and extraordinary. As a husband, father, friend; ordinary. As a mentor to the world; extraordinary.

This past month I've once again been traveling, sharing the Principles in Britain and Spain. During my speaking engagements at various venues, a couple of things really stirred me.

One is how deeply people are moved by Syd's story. Each time I speak about his Enlightenment and the historical relevance it has for the mental health of humanity, the feeling becomes more powerful. People weep, filled with the emotion of hope and the possibility of an answer to life's dilemmas. In that moment, insights are born that transform lives. There is a spiritual mystery taking place that transcends the norm.

The second thing I noticed is that there is a cyclical effect occurring in second and third generation practitioners who are serving in many of the same areas where first generation practitioners introduced the Principles forty years ago.

For example, Dr. Roger Mills, one of the first two psychologists to study with Syd, became a pioneer in bringing the Principles understanding to inner city communities, resulting in great success. I was so inspired by the residents I met from that first community project in Modello public housing in Miami, that I began to work with Roger to develop programs and research tools to serve these communities across America.

Now I see second and third generation practitioners doing the same thing; not only aiding inner city communities, but also serving in prisons, education, business, working with youth, and much more. So many human endeavors are being helped by new practitioners trained in the Principles.

As I met many of the new service providers in my travels, I was inspired by their passion, and their dedication to helping others. They in turn, were surprised to learn they were following in first generation footsteps, as many were unaware of this. Sharing stories fostered a new level of understanding and respect for what each generation is bringing to the table.

It also tells me that the Principles paradigm introduced by Sydney Banks over four decades ago is sustainable; each generation contributing further to the mental health of the world.

Before Syd's passing, he reassured those of us who wondered if the integrity of his message would remain true, after he was gone. Certainly, he himself had some concerns about the commercialization he saw of the Principles as a product.

Still, Syd never lost his faith that the Principles themselves would continue to flourish in the world, long after he was gone, and after we, the first generation are gone. How can you contaminate formless spiritual essence?

The Principles underlying the human experience can never be damaged and will last for eternity. To me, this offers unlimited hope for humanity and for our planet.

Resources

http://www.sydbanks.com/
Syd's available resources

www.sydneybanks.org
Syd's website is archived

www.3phd.net
3 Principles for Human Development, Elsie's website

www.threeprinciplesfoundation.org
Hosts the Three Principles School

Your own wisdom!

Made in the USA
Columbia, SC
14 March 2018